EDUCATION FOR CHRISTIAN LIVING

EDUCATION FOR CHRISTIAN LIVING

Strategies for Nurture Based on Biblical and Historical Foundations

MARVIN L. ROLOFF
EDITOR

AUGSBURG Publishing House • Minneapolis

EDUCATION FOR CHRISTIAN LIVING
Strategies for Nurture Based on Biblical and Historical Foundations

Library of Congress Cataloging-in-Publication Data

EDUCATION FOR CHRISTIAN LIVING.

   Bibliography: p.
   1. Christian education. I. Roloff, Marvin L., 1934–
BV1471.2.E28   1987   86-28756
ISBN 0-8066-2238-5

Manufactured in the U.S.A.   APH 10-2003

1 2 3 4 5 6 7 8 9 0 1 2 3 4 5 6 7 8 9

CONTENTS

PREFACE

Education for Christian Living is a unique book written by professors of Christian education at seminaries from the American Lutheran Church, Evangelical Lutheran Church in Canada, and Lutheran Church in America. These professors are:

JEAN BOZEMAN
Lutheran School of Theology
Chicago, Illinois

ERWIN BUCK
Lutheran Theological Seminary
Saskatoon, Saskatchewan

ROBERT L. CONRAD
Lutheran School of Theology
Chicago, Illinois

DONALD L. DEFFNER
Pacific Lutheran Theological Seminary
Berkeley, California

NORMA J. EVERIST
Wartburg Theological Seminary
Dubuque, Iowa

A. ROGER GOBBEL
Lutheran Theological Seminary
Gettysburg, Pennsylvania

MARY E. HUGHES
Trinity Lutheran Seminary
Columbus, Ohio

KENT L. JOHNSON
Luther Northwestern Theological Seminary
St. Paul, Minnesota

EUGENE C. KREIDER
Luther Northwestern Theological Seminary
St. Paul, Minnesota

MARGARET A. KRYCH
Lutheran Theological Seminary
Philadelphia, Pennsylvania

HAROLD F. PARK
Lutheran Theological Southern Seminary
Columbia, South Carolina

ARNOLD D. WEIGEL
Waterloo Lutheran Seminary
Waterloo, Ontario

This book is representative of Lutheran Christian education teaching in North America. The book is a result of annual meetings of these professors. At several meetings they discussed the possibilities of writing a textbook that would represent their collective thinking and that all could use in education classes and congregations. After submitting suggestions for subjects to be addressed in such a book, each agreed to write a chapter. The outcome appears on the following pages.

We thank God for faithful teachers throughout the church, and particularly for these men and women who teach at its seminaries.

INTRODUCTION

Marvin L. Roloff

Time has the qualities of past, present, and future. The three are sometimes so closely connected that we find it difficult even to comprehend time's passage. But the future is constantly slipping into the past, and it is in this transitory present moment that Christian living takes place.

The links between the past, present, and future are especially meaningful to Christians living within the fellowship of those who believe in Christ the Savior. The Christ who came 2000 years ago is present in everyday life and is also the hope of the future.

Christians confront a constantly changing world, and they need to cope with this change. Just when we think we have coped with yesterday, today brings new challenges for tomorrow. Education for Christian living enables believers to live with faith and hope in a world of threat and change.

Education is the process in which learning and teaching takes place. It is bringing the gospel of Jesus Christ to someone who has already heard the good news. This may sound peculiar to some, but if we consider the work of the church today, we discover that there is both *mission* and *education*. *Mission* is introducing someone to God and to the good news of salvation through Jesus Christ; *education* is bringing the good news to those who have already heard.

Three biblical texts summarize the tasks of education for Christian living today.

In 2 Peter 3:18 we are encouraged to ". . . grow in the grace and knowledge of our Lord and Savior Jesus Christ." This implies daily growth to meet the needs and challenges of Christian living.

9

At the same time, John 10:10 reminds us that Jesus came that we might have life and have it abundantly. Jesus wants our lives to be abundant in our relationships with him and with others.

Finally, in Luke 18:8, Jesus posed the question: ". . . when the Son of man comes, will he find faith on earth?" It's a poignant question for today. Surely the Son of man will find many religions and material things, but will he find faith?

This book on education for Christian living carries our heritage from the past into life and reflects it in a vision for the future, but it is done in the context of Christian living. We are reminded that we are added to the past, carried into the future, and that we live today in the grace of Christian living.

Christian Education in the Church

Education has always been a passion for the people of God. From earliest records of the Hebrews in the Old Testament, education was an important function. Hebrew parents were instructed to teach their children.

Likewise, in the New Testament church, education was central. The story of Jesus Christ added zeal to the early Christians to help others learn more about the great teacher and Savior who came to die so that all might have eternal life. Also, the task of equipping the saints is clearly outlined in the New Testament letters. The apostle Paul is remembered as one of the earliest teachers who followed Christ.

A rich history of Christian education continues from the time of the New Testament church to the present. Overcoming barriers, the message of God's gift of salvation to all has been passed from generation to generation by committed teachers and preachers of the Word.

Education for Christian Living provides a unique look at education, particularly in Lutheran churches in North America. Christian education has always held a priority for the many Lutherans who emigrated from northern Europe to the United States and Canada. Arriving in this new country, they brought with them their Bibles, hymnbooks and catechisms. The tradition has continued. Even today, Lutherans consider the Bible, hymnal, and catechism primary resources for Christian education. There is hardly a Lutheran congregation in this country that does not have educational facilities and a program of Christian education for all ages and needs. Sunday schools and vacation schools abound, confirmation classes are assumed, youth learning continues, and new adult education programs become more and more popular. Committed lay leaders and pastors continue the heritage of learning by developing new resources for contemporary needs and training leaders to develop new strategies.

Significant changes have occurred in education in recent decades. Educators have long had a history of catching fads, thinking they are immediate solutions to new problems. They have also learned that fads don't always solve all problems, but almost all of them do stimulate some kind of positive growth in congregations.

Trends in Christian Education

The following education trends have developed in congregations during the past years:

1. Biblical learning

Within the past 15 or 20 years there has been an increased emphasis on Bible learning. After the 1960s, with its attention to social issues and unrest, congregational leaders sensed that parishioners felt unable to deal with the issues without a biblical base. Nurture seemed to have lost its foundation, leaving people floundering without an anchor of faith. Now there is a desire to return to biblical roots.

2. Expanded scope of biblical context

Movements of inclusivity have opened the eyes of educators to include more Bible content than has ever been taught, particularly regarding women. After centuries of focusing on stories containing primarily men, scripture texts were selected that also included women or references to them. This will have long-range implications for young children who are nurtured in a faith that is more inclusive in its context. Leadership in congregations will see that God has called both male and female persons as instruments of outreach and service in the church.

3. New approaches and educational methodologies

In keeping with the increased concern for communication in the world at all levels, educators have introduced new approaches and methodologies in teaching and learning. In addition, educators in Christian education have become more sensitive to the variety of ways students learn. They no longer assume that all people learn best by reading. Therefore new approaches of sensory and experiential learning have been applied in Christian education, with positive results.

Teachers' guides offer optional teaching approaches and a variety of ways for introducing new learnings and learning reinforcements. In addition, various kinds of teacher education have helped teachers in Christian education to acquire new skills.

Trends are still in process for the most effective utilization of media and high technology in Christian education. Both Christian educators and resource developers are seeking to find ways new media can best be utilized in the church.

4. Curriculum in the congregation

A significant change in curriculum development has occurred in recent years. Congregations have become more intentional in selecting resources that assist them in meeting their needs and becoming the curriculum for their congregation. Two significant things have happened as a result of this. First, congregations become much more "education oriented." Leaders in congregations set goals for educational ministry and discover their own particular needs. Then they examine resources for their theological, educational, social, and congregational content and choose those that can best nurture the life of their congregation.

On the other hand, national developers of resources, for either media or training events for leaders, have changed from providing a fixed program for congregations to accept to providing optional styles and approaches, so congregations can be selective and choose those resources that best meet their needs.

Not only does this keep resources more current, because congregations are continuing their search for resources, it also causes a congregation to evaluate its education program more frequently. This whole shift of perspective has caused congregations to develop stronger leaders and become more discerning in their selection of resources.

5. Broader vision of nurture

Though the definitions of Christian nurture vary, nurture generally is viewed as being involved and included in a Christian community. The image that is most common is of a plant that is planted, nourished, and grows. Within recent years educators have become more intentional about the aspects of nurture, so that teaching and learning include more than the acquisition of knowledge and information. Christian nurture looks not only at learning the elements of faith but also at ways of articulating the faith in Christian living throughout society. Christian nurture looks at Christian learning and relates it to teaching, fellowship, worship, outreach, and service. Returning to the image of the plant, nurture means the plant will not only grow, but also produce flowers or fruits that are shared and used.

This broader vision of nurture has not diminished the place of learning, but has added a new dimension that has not been prominent in Lutheran tradition. New Bible study programs that have encouraged witness and worship have produced amazing stories from people who have learned and witnessed to one another. For many, talking about the meaning of faith in their Christian living has been a new experience.

6. Inclusivity and language

In its teaching and learning, education has become sensitive to the inclusivity of God's people and the language used in expressing the faith in an inclusive church. This has implications for viewing the Word of God, the relationships in the world, and Christian living in the congregation.

Language used in resources is careful in making personal references to God, being faithful to theological convictions but aware of male/female sensitivities. Likewise, offensive language is avoided in areas of race, sex, handicaps, age, and other sensitive topics. Guidelines for avoiding bias have been prepared by denominations to assist persons in their use of language.

The church's response to inclusive language concerns is evident in worship materials, hymns, and education resources. Congregational leaders examine resources closely with criteria for inclusivity.

Strategies to Meet Today's Issues

A distinction needs to be made between Christian living, Christian education, and education in the church. Christian education is education in the church for Christian living built on the gospel message of Jesus Christ. Christian educators ask, "How do you nurture someone?" or, "How am I nurtured in my own Christian faith and life?" In these processes there are issues to be addressed by leaders in education as they seek to establish a climate for Christian living.

1. Centrality of the gospel

Education for Christian living is organized around the gospel message of Jesus Christ. Experiences of teaching and learning assist persons to understand who Jesus Christ is and to respond to the grace of Christ in their relationships with others. Though education systems can be organized around many other legitimate principles such as the catechism, learner experiences, Baptism, etc., the ultimate purpose is to develop a closer relationship with Christ in life.

2. God-given resources

In Christian education God provides the resources of the Holy Spirit, time, people, and experience. Christian education cannot be viewed outside the context of the presence of the Holy Spirit. God provides the time, whether it be in preparation of a session, personal reflection, or group learning. People in education include learner and teacher together. Finally, the experience of Christian fellowship is a gift of God to be treasured.

3. Needs of a changing world

Christian educators cannot develop strategies for nurture apart from society and culture. Influences and pressures of a culture produce needs of the society, individually and collectively. One of the most profound tasks of Christian living is to deal with the tension of living in a culture that is not Christian. It is necessary to ask what Christian living is and where it takes place. Educators need to weigh the implications of Christian education in a society that has become more and more pluralistic.

How do the values of Christian living become expressed and felt in a world of changing values and standards. Christian educators constantly ask, "Does Christian living make any difference in the world?"

4. The Bible

Holy Scripture contains the magnificent story of God's grace and love for the world and the response of God's people. This story is the continuum that runs through Christian living. The Bible is a means through which God's Word is made known to us. It remains the primary sourcebook for Christian faith.

5. The body of Christ

The apostle Paul described the church as the body of Christ. This image incorporates both the individual and corporate aspects of the church. Together we are the body of Christ, yet separately I exist as a child of God. This creative tension of the individual and the corporate always exists within the body. We cannot live without one another. Therefore, the question for Christian living is, How can we be Christian together?

6. Family

Home and family have long provided the basic fabric for Christian living. Today educators need to examine recent changes in home and family life to discover implications for Christian education. It is vital that new ways be developed for awakening religious consciousness in the home.

7. Method and content

Unless care is taken, an unnecessary conflict between method and content can arise. The educator who cares only about content may discover that without process no one will ever understand the message.

On the other hand, an educator who cares only about process may find learning to be a great experience but without content. An appropriate balance is essential to teaching and learning.

8. Teacher education

Educators need education. Ongoing teacher education has a two-sided benefit. On the one side, ongoing training assists the teacher in utilizing skills that will help the learner. On the other side, it will help the teacher develop positive self-worth that results from a good teaching experience. Because learner needs change within society and congregations, new approaches are needed for ongoing teacher education.

The Heritage and the Future

How does a congregation respond to the ongoing needs of members who are living in a high-tech, pluralistic society? Strategies suggested in this book are based on biblical and historical foundations. The heritage of Lutheran education carries many strengths that have endured through generations. These strengths allow for changes in approaches and methodologies to meet the changes brought by a new age.

Each chapter of this book looks at a separate aspect of the educational process, following a sequence that first examines the heritage and then projects into the future. Together the chapters present a strategy of education for Christian living.

The congregation is central to Christian education in the Lutheran church. In Chapter 1, Robert L. Conrad traces the roots of Christian education in North American congregational life back to Jewish and early Christian education. This early education supports the idea that first adults are taught and then they in turn instruct their children. This chapter also considers the contributions of the Reformation to Christian education. Martin Luther emphasized that learning should relate to daily life, and this emphasis still influences our practical methodology. Luther's influence continued in Europe and with the immigrants who settled in North America.

Chapter 2 is a key chapter for developing strategies for nurture. Here Eugene C. Kreider describes the work of Christian education and offers foundations for doing it. He explains how the Bible, theology, and the social sciences are the foundations for Christian education. The work of Christian education is a living tradition from past to future, a theme carried over from Chapter 1. Kreider moves with a central objective for Christian education that is applicable to all within a given community of faith. Helps for developing strategies are included through an understanding of goals and objectives used in Christian education.

In Chapter 3, Jean Bozeman demonstrates nurture through the community of faith, using Deuteronomy 6:4-9 as a model of a learning community. The purpose of the learning community is to understand the gospel for ourselves and to share the news with others. She describes this community as one of hope, joy, and new life. This community undergirds other functions in the congregation including worship, witness, and support to the mission of God's people.

Chapter 4 continues to develop the strategy for the community of faith. Here Norma Everist states that the community of faith is the curriculum: God and God's people in this time and place. The center of this community is Christ present in each member of the community through Baptism. This is foundational for Christian living. Everist states that the learning environment is the entire culture in which we live. A part of this culture is the learning environment, including a law-and-gospel dimension. "The world in which we live shapes us," and this provides a connection between culture and God's Word. By being aware of the Bible tradition, cultural influence, and learners' experience, teachers can choose appropriate methods to accomplish objectives within strategies for nurture.

In Chapter 5, Erwin Buck explores the interaction of faith and culture and introduces the concept of value systems in Christian living. The central question is, Does culture shape one's faith or does one's faith shape one's culture?

In Chapter 6, Donald L. Deffner defines evangelization as the activity of bringing the gospel of salvation in Jesus Christ to people everywhere. A careful analysis of the educated adult offers implications for the church's ministry of evangelism and education.

Margaret A. Krych begins Chapter 7 by saying that learning about and responding to the good news of God's mercy and forgiveness in Jesus Christ is a lifelong process. She urges educators to consider the human development of each individual from birth through adulthood. She also stresses the balance between cognitive information and emotional and social learning in teaching the gospel.

In Chapter 8, "Christian Education: An Exercise in Interpreting," A. Roger Gobbel speaks of interpretation as an ongoing, lifelong task in which children, adolescents, and adults participate. Participation in the activity of interpretation and the results of that activity are determined by developmental abilities and limitations (building on the principles of Chapter 7). Interpretation is a personal and unique trait. Each person interprets in a different way.

In Chapter 9, Kent Johnson proposes a Lutheran approach to teaching. He brings worship and education together, using the liturgy as an approach to teaching. Both education and liturgy affirm the community of faith as the people of God and challenge the participants to be servants of God in the world.

In Chapter 10, Mary E. Hughes examines five functions of administration of Christian education in a congregation. These functions relate to all the other strategies for education for Christian living.

Chapter 11 deals with the strategy of leadership in Christian education. Harold Park examines the role of leadership in educational ministry, with a specific look at the role of the pastor.

In the final chapter, Arnold D. Weigel projects strategies for nurture into the future. He underscores the premise that the congregation is a basic locus for Christian nurture and ministry, considering internal growth and outreach centered in the congregation's worship life.

Our challenge is to bring the past, present, and future together so that today's church *is* the future, as the body of believers responds to God's call.

ONE

ROOTS OF CHRISTIAN EDUCATION IN NORTH AMERICA

Robert L. Conrad

An examination of the roots of Christian education for Lutheran churches begins with the earliest roots, Jewish and early Christian education. Jewish education focused on careful instruction in the *Torah* (Law) as the basic content and on the family, later supplemented by Sabbath schools, as the basic agency. Christianity was born in this context and, as a minority religion, also had to depend on careful instruction in the family and faith community to maintain itself in the face of persecution. Early Christianity developed a thorough system of preparation for Baptism, a system that broke down when Constantine made Christianity the religion of the state (A.D. 313–330).

Education of the members of the church did not fare well for many centuries, depending mostly on the use of ritual, symbol, and art. At the time of the Reformation there was an emphasis on the education of all people in order that they might know the basics of the Christian faith and be able to carry out their calling as Christians in the world. Luther wrote the *Large* and *Small Catechism* to help parents and pastors teach children, but he also proposed communal schools for training people in all the skills necessary to carry out their calling and maintain the civil state.

In his concept of the Christian's calling, Luther provides Lutherans with the greatest of all educational challenges—how to equip young people for their calling as Christians in the world without isolating them from the world, on the one hand, or losing them to the world, on the other. It is the same struggle that earlier communities of faith have had, and the history of Lutheranism shows that it has had varying success in its attempts to meet the challenge.

The Reformation era was succeeded by orthodoxy, rationalism, and pietism, all of which had their influences on what Lutheran immigrants brought to the United States. All Lutherans tried to pass on the faith, especially through the use of catechisms and the rite of confirmation. Many Lutherans adopted the American pattern of public school and Sunday school as the way in which to carry on Christian education. Others adopted parochial schools and fended off the Sunday school for a long time. But regardless of their choice of educational agency, Lutherans tried to equip young people for the Christian calling through the use of tried and true instruments like the catechisms and the rite of confirmation.

At the end of this chapter is a summation of the implications to be drawn from this examination of the history of Christian education in Lutheranism.

Jewish Education

As in most ancient civilizations, Israelite education during the early biblical period was family-oriented. Learning took place by means of face-to-face relationships during the course of daily family activities. The first way in which a child in an Israelite home learned was by participation in the activities of the family. A second way was by the father's instruction in the codes of living (later embodied in the Hebrew Scriptures). Children were to learn and conduct themselves according to the instructions for daily living preserved in such books as Exodus, Leviticus, and Deuteronomy. A third way children learned was through the oral tradition that spoke of the will of God in history and in law. Children were told of the mighty acts of God on behalf of God's people in the past. They were also told the Law of God as it had been taught to God's people in the course of their history. Deuteronomy 6:4-9, the

Shema ("Hear, O Israel"), relates the importance of teaching the Law of God to children at many times and in many ways.[1]

Children also learned through participation in the rituals of their nation and family. The curiosity of children was aroused through participation, prompting them to ask about the meaning of such rituals. This gave parents the opportunity to explain why they observed the ritual. There were many rituals in the life of the Jewish child and family. Each male child was to be circumcised eight days after birth. Forty days after birth the mother had to go through the ritual of purification. There were articles of apparel to be worn, such as the phylacteries—two small leather boxes, one worn on the arm and the other on the head, each containing four scripture passages. At 13 the Jewish boy celebrated his *bar mitzvah*, which means "son of the commandment." The whole family would observe Sabbath, Passover, and the Feast of Tabernacles. Passover was a celebration of freedom, and the Feast of Tabernacles, at least in part, was a celebration of the Law.[2]

Conditions changed for the Israelites with the Babylonian captivity. The learning and keeping of the *Torah* gained heightened significance, for only those who faithfully kept the *Torah* would survive. The theme of a saved remnant became prominent, especially as proclaimed by Ezekiel, a prophet of the Exile. And, although its origins are not entirely known, the synagogue may well have originated during the Exile. Its purpose was teaching—teaching the *Torah*.

The *Torah* was in both written and oral form. The written form was the Scriptures of the Pentateuch, the five books of Moses. The oral form was that of the *Mishnah*, the interpretation of the Scriptures, and the interpretation of the *Mishnah*, the *Talmud* (the study). There was also a moral interpretation called the *Midrash*.

It was imperative that children learn the written and oral *Torah*. Fathers were to begin teaching the *Torah* to their children at age four. By age 13, children were to assume adult responsibilities in the Israelite community. This meant that fathers were to teach the Hebrew language as well as the content and character of *Torah*.

Because it was difficult for fathers to carry out their responsibilities, schools came into existence to help in teaching the *Torah*. Their origin is obscure. The earliest reference to them occurs in 75 B.C.[3] The schools for children were connected with the synagogue and were called *Beth Hassapher* (House of the Book). Their main focus was the teaching of Hebrew and the written *Torah,* the Scriptures. They are the fore-runners of today's Sabbath schools. There were some schools of higher learning, secondary schools, that were called *Beth Hammidrash* (House of Interpretation) or *Beth Talmud,* (House of Study). A respected teach-er would gather students for the study of oral *Torah,* the *Mishnah.* In both the elementary and secondary schools the Jewish concern to learn and obey the *Torah* was foremost.

The results of a thorough Jewish education was a people who knew their language and their law, both written and oral. They tried to protect themselves against being swallowed up by the surrounding cultures. To a great extent they succeeded, but it was a constant struggle, es-pecially for Jews who were scattered to other lands. The fact that the Old Testament was translated into Greek in the Septuagint is proof enough that the native tongue and teaching were at risk. However, their educational system was flexible enough to adapt itself to changing and challenging circumstances. The Jewish people and their education sur-vive to this day.

Early Christian Education

As a Jew, Jesus undoubtedly attended Sabbath school and studied the Scriptures. It is also likely that Joseph and Mary educated him in the ways of the children of Israel. He certainly held his own at age 12 in what must have been a version of the *Beth Talmud,* the House of Study. As he grew, Jesus was primarily known as *Rabbi,* Teacher.

In the New Testament there is evidence of a two-step process in the making of believers practiced by Jesus and the disciples. First was the speaking of the *kerygma,* the proclamation of what God had done in Jesus Christ. Then came the *didache,* the teaching to those who became followers of Jesus. There were several types of teaching. The first was an interpretation of the Hebrew Scriptures. A second was the teaching of the Tradition, in this case, the early Christian tradition. Confessions of faith were the third type of teaching. Such confessions (such as the Old Roman Symbol, the predecessor of the Apostles' Creed) were taught especially to those who were to be baptized. The life and sayings of Jesus were a fourth type. The last type was instruction in the two ways of life, that is, the way of life and the way of death.[4]

The family also played an important part in education in the early Christian church. The New Testament indicates that whole families were converted, and the children of these families needed instruction in the Christian faith. Ephesians speaks of the responsibility of fathers to bring their children up in the *paideia* of the Lord (Eph. 6:4). *Paideia* was the Greek concept that conveyed the notion of passing on the whole of a culture's traditions. Christian fathers were to educate their children in the tradition of the Christian faith. It was to be done "in the Lord," and it included all the teachings of the Christian faith.

While there is little evidence as to the nature of the instruction that parents gave children, there is a great deal of evidence about the type of instruction that developed for adults who became members of the early Christian church. It was a process of *catechesis* (meaning, "to sound down") or oral instruction in the faith. During the first three centuries of Christian history instruction in the faith could take as long as three years. Persons who wanted to join the church first had to present themselves to the bishop, who would conduct a lengthy inquiry into their background and morals. They would usually be accompanied by sponsors, who were already members of the church. After the candidates had passed the initial examination, they were admitted to the class of "hearers" (*audientes*). They could attend the first part of the worship service, the *missa catechumenorum* (mass of the catechumens), but had to leave before the celebration of the Eucharist, the *missa fidelium* (mass of the faithful), reserved for church members. They had weekly instruction in the rudiments of the faith, including Scripture, church history, the Lord's Prayer, the Ten Commandments, and the sacraments. During the last intensive weeks of preparation prior to their Baptism at Easter, the candidates were called *competentes*. The period of time in which the candidates were intensively prepared for Baptism became the basis for the season of Lent. At the end of the time of preparation, at midnight on Easter eve, the candidates were baptized and brought into the company of the faithful.[5] This catechetical process allowed for careful instruction in the Christian faith prior to Baptism and resulted in followers who were informed and committed.

Everything changed when Christianity became the religion of the state under Constantine. Hordes of people joined the church, and instruction for membership was nearly impossible. The rites that had been a meaningful part of the previous instruction now became shortened rituals. And by the fifth century, when almost everyone was baptized as an infant, the catechumenate became postbaptismal instruction leading to confirmation.

Even that instruction became minimal during the following centuries as education of the members centered less on the use of word and more on the use of symbol in sacrament, liturgy, art, and drama. The use of sound, light, color, and image is a powerful way to teach, but during the Middle Ages the common people had little verbal or written instruction. Significant instruction in the Christian faith was reserved for the clergy and for those in the universities.[6]

Contributions of the Reformation to Christian Education

At the time of the Reformation, Martin Luther and the other reformers felt that education was a necessity for all the people, not just the clergy and those in the universities. Education for everyone was important for both spiritual and secular reasons. It was imperative that parents and pastors learn the basics of the Christian faith and pass them on to the children. But it was also essential that people be educated so that they could carry out their calling as Christians in the structures of society.

The primary responsibility for education was given to parents. Luther said that it was God's command that parents make certain their children were educated. That command is found in Psalm 78:5-6, Deuteronomy 32:7, and the Fourth Commandment. "Indeed," Luther said, "for what purpose do we older folks exist, other than to care for, instruct and bring up the young? . . . This is why God has entrusted them to us who are older and know from experience what is best for them. And God holds us strictly accountable for them."[7] The head of each household was especially responsible for the religious education of the children. The subtitle of each section of the *Small Catechism* reads, "in the plain form in which the head of the family shall teach them to his household."

However, Luther had no illusions that parents were able to do the job all by themselves. Bishops and pastors were also to be responsible for the religious education of the children of their parishes. In his letter to bishops and pastors that accompanied the 1529 publication of the *Small Catechism,* Luther deplored the state of religious knowledge of the people.

> The deplorable conditions which I recently encountered when I was a visitor constrained me to prepare this brief and simple catechism or statement of Christian teaching. Good God, what wretchedness I beheld! The common people, especially those who live in the country, have no knowledge whatever of Christian teaching, and unfortunately many pastors are quite incompetent and unfitted for teaching. . . .
>
> I therefore beg you for God's sake, my beloved brethren who are pastors and preachers, that you take the duties of your office seriously, that you have pity on the people who are entrusted to your care, and that you help me to teach the catechism to the people, especially those who are young.[8]

Luther also called on government officials to see to the education of children, especially in public education. Parents had a difficult enough time with the religious education of their children, Luther said, and it was almost impossible for them to take care of their secular education. In a 1524 letter to mayors and councilmen of German cities, he cited three reasons why parents could not do the job: (1) They lacked the piety to do it; (2) they weren't qualified and didn't know how; and (3), even if they wanted to educate their children, they didn't have the time.[9] Since parents couldn't educate their children themselves, the most important thing they could do was send them to school.

In 1530 Luther wrote a sermon on the importance of sending children to school, emphasizing both the spiritual and temporal importance of education. The spiritual aspect centered on the need for pastors, and pastors came only from those who were willing to see that their sons were educated for the ministry.[10] The temporal need centered on the necessity of maintaining civil government, a divinely ordained office that required the best possible persons. In fact, Luther went so far as to say that more ability is required for civil office than for the ministry.

Indeed, there is need in this office for abler people than are needed in
the office of preaching, so it is necessary to get the best boys for this
work; for in the preaching office Christ does the whole thing, by His
Spirit, but in the worldly kingdom men must act on the basis of reason.
. . . He has not sent the Holy Spirit from heaven for this purpose. This
is why to govern temporally is harder, because conscience cannot rule;
one must act, so to speak, in the dark.[11]

But schools were needed for the common people as well, not just
for those who governed. In his letter to the mayors and councilmen
Luther said they should establish schools to assure the welfare, safety,
and strength of the whole city, and that was best done by having able,
wise, and educated citizens.

Now if (as we have assumed) there were no souls, and there were no
need at all of schools and languages for the sake of the Scriptures and
of God, this one consideration alone would be sufficient to justify the
establishment everywhere of the very best schools for both boys and
girls, namely, that in order to maintain its temporal estate outwardly the
world must have good and capable men and women, men able to rule
well over land people, women able to manage the household and train
children and servants aright. Now such men must come from our boys,
and such women from our girls. Therefore, it is a matter of properly
educating and training our boys and girls to that end.[12]

Though a man of his time in the way he saw the roles of men and
women, Luther was ahead of his time in making a case for universal
education for girls as well as boys.

To some people, Luther's reasoning that schools were valuable for
both spiritual and secular reasons seems a confusing mixture of Christian education and secular education.[13] But Luther could combine the
two because he believed that Christians lived in both Christ's kingdom
and the kingdom of this world, and they were called to live responsibly
in both kingdoms.

The believer is called by the Holy Spirit to a life of divine forgiveness
and fellowship in the church. This primary calling of the Christian is
clearly spelled out in Luther's explanation to the Third Article. "I
believe that by my own reason or strength I cannot believe in Jesus

Christ, my Lord, or come to him. But the Holy Ghost has called me through the Gospel, enlightened me with his gifts, and sanctified and preserved me in true faith." [14]

This primary calling is accompanied by a corollary calling. God calls all those who are forgiven and who live in the fellowship of the church to a life of loving service in all their relationships. [15] Every Christian has a vocation, a calling (*Beruf,* in Luther's terminology), that is to be carried out in the Christian's station (*Stand*) or office (*Amt* or *Stelle*). [16] The church of his day had taught that only the clergy had a calling, but Luther emphasized that every Christian had a calling and a place in life in which there were opportunities for service. That service took place in the ordinary structures of life such as the family and the state. Such structures were the "masks of God" in which God was both hidden and yet revealed as he made his will known to people. [17]

People are needed to fill and adequately carry out the responsibilities of offices in the structures of everyday existence. Luther insisted that the offices be open to all qualified persons and, therefore, education should be available to all, not just to the nobility. "It is not God's will that only those who are born kings, princes, lords, and nobles should exercise rule and lordship. He wills to have his beggars among them also." [18] So Luther's argument came full circle when he insisted that secular education was needed to make it possible for people to carry out their calling by God within the structures of everyday life.

Aside from a rationale for education that included both sacred and secular elements, Luther made other contributions to education in the 16th century. As has already been noted, he was ahead of his time in insisting on compulsory education for both boys and girls. The state not only had the responsibility of providing education for children, but it also had the duty to enforce participation. Many parents in Luther's day resisted sending their children to school because they wanted them to learn how to make a living and contribute to the family welfare. Knowing this, Luther proposed part-time education, in which boys would go to school one or two hours a day and girls would go one hour a day. [19] But while part-time education was suitable for ordinary students, superior students should have full-time, extended education. "The exceptional pupils, who give promise of becoming skilled teachers, preachers, or holders of other ecclesiastical positions, should be allowed to continue in school longer, or even be dedicated to a life of study."[20] A structured and somewhat elite education for exceptional students was another of Luther's unique contributions to education in general.[21]

Besides contributions to the educational systems of his day Luther also contributed ideas for learning method. He wanted children to learn through a Socratic method of asking questions and eliciting answers rather than slavish adherence to authority. He wanted children to experience the joy of learning, and he urged those responsible for education to take advantage of the natural activity and inquisitiveness of children. He tried to use things observed in everyday life as educational tools rather than stiff abstractions. He was aware of and emphasized the learning community, that is, the interrelatedness of people in learning. And Luther's love of music led him to emphasize that teachers be able to use music in the education of the young.[22]

Luther made another contribution to learning that he probably was not aware of. This involved the way he came to a new understanding of his relation to God. He came to understand God through insight rather than logic. Luther's insights came through his experience of *Anfechtung,* his struggle with God.

Luther's basic struggle involved his desire to find a gracious God, because all he had found was a judging God who held him accountable for his failure to attain righteousness. Luther had been taught that a person could do the will of God well enough so that God would grant grace to attain a state of righteousness, but he found he could not do the will of God at all. He said that he hated God because of the impossible demand made on him for a righteousness he could not attain. He meditated on what Paul said in Romans 1:17, where he maintained that the righteous shall live by faith. When Luther realized that righteousness is a gift that faith receives, and not a demand that cannot be met, he felt as if he had been born again and had entered paradise. He could then connect and explain many other elements of his theology in the light of this new insight.[23]

Luther's experience involved a four-step learning process. The first was the struggle of his *Anfechtung,* which involved a logically irreconcilable conflict. God demanded a righteousness that Luther could not attain. The second step was meditation, pondering, or silence (to use Luther's words), in which the struggle was left to percolate in the inner recesses of the mind. Third, came the experience of a new insight: righteousness was a gift, not a demand. The relief and wonder of it all had a ripple effect. Luther then understood the gospel as offering a gift which faith receives. The fourth step was the interpretation of the new insight and all that it meant for the believer. Luther filled many volumes as he interpreted to others what he had come to know.[24] The contribution Luther made as an insightful learner is explored in the last section of this chapter.

Luther did not have much immediate impact on the system of schools in Germany. But he did influence what parents and pastors did by way of instruction of the young for confirmation, especially through his catechisms. A series of sermons that Luther preached on the chief parts of the Christian faith were published in April 1529, in what became known as the *Large Catechism*. Pastors found its content suitable for both preaching and teaching in the parish. That was followed in May of the same year with a short version which had originally been published as a set of posters. The *Small Catechism* became the handbook for teaching the young. In Germany it was published in several regional dialects. The same was true for some sections of Poland, the Baltic countries, and Hungary. By the end of the 16th century it had been translated into virtually every European language.[25]

In the 16th century, confirmation instruction was primarily the responsibility of the home, with pastors aiding in catechetical instruction at the church.[26] Pastors used the *Small Catechism* in the *Kinderlehre* (the "children's teaching"), the equivalent of today's confirmation instruction or Sunday school. They worked with the candidates in order to be assured that the young people were ready for first communion. Confirmation took place at an earlier age and in a much less formal way than is the present practice.

Post-Reformation Trends

Over time, confirmation was affected by various theological trends, becoming more formal and important in the eyes of pastors and parents. Confirmation instruction also became part of the school system. The first theological trend to affect an understanding of confirmation was 17th-century Lutheran orthodoxy. There was a tendency to spell out all possible theological ramifications in the catechisms and to require that catechumens go over and over the material in a dull and repetitious manner. Catechetical instruction and confirmation became quite formal.[27]

The reaction against orthodoxy was the pietism of the late 17th and early 18th centuries. Philip Jacob Spener, a Lutheran pastor in Frankfurt, wanted the catechumens to personally experience their faith and to use the catechism as a devotional aid. Confirmation became the occasion for the catechumen to ratify the baptismal covenant, to give witness to personal faith or "conversion," and to accept the obligation to lead a Christian life.[28] Up to this time confirmation was a matter of concern for the church, but now it became a personal and subjective concern. Because the catechumen had to be able to practice self-examination, it became necessary to extend the age of confirmation. Whereas confirmation had previously been at age 12, now it was delayed until 14 or older.

Eighteenth-century rationalism was the third theological trend to influence confirmation. Rationalism emphasized the ability of human reason to grasp religious truth. Whereas pietism stressed experience, rationalism stressed reason. Catechumens were to be intellectually active in the learning process, and pastors were to tailor their instruction to the ability of the candidates. At the same time, rationalism attached such great importance to an intellectually-oriented confirmation that the meaning and importance of Baptism was overshadowed. Confirmation became the second half of Baptism—indeed, the more important half. It made one a member of the church and was celebrated with much fanfare. Rationalism affected the content of the catechisms. The theology of catechisms published in the age of rationalism was far different from that of Martin Luther.[29]

The 19th century brought a reaction to the theology of rationalism in the form of a "church revival" in the 1830s. The revival emphasized the Bible and the church's tradition in the education and transformation of church members. It sparked a new interest in catechetical instruction, in Luther's *Small Catechism,* and in new explanations of the catechism. One such explanation was published by Wilhelm Loehe, a pastor who had great influence on German Lutheranism in America.[30]

As confirmation moved farther and farther from parental instruction and into an extended, formal rite in the church, the responsibility for instruction moved from the home to the school. By the 19th century the German system of schooling had incorporated instruction for confirmation. Children attended the *Volksschule,* the community elementary school. The school was not secular in the modern sense, but reflected the confessional stance of the community, either Lutheran or Roman Catholic. Instruction for confirmation was part of the curriculum of the school. Graduation and confirmation were one and the same thing; a boy or girl could not leave school without being confirmed. That usually occurred at age 14; in some areas the age was even higher. Many children would end their formal schooling at this point and become apprentices in order to learn a trade.

Others would enter either the *Gymnasium* or the *Realgymnasium* for six to nine additional years. The *Gymnasium* consisted of courses that accented the professional languages: Latin, Greek, and Hebrew. Students who wanted to go on into law, medicine, or theology were required to take the same course of study. When they successfully passed their examinations, they could continue their professional preparation at a university. The *Realgymnasium* had fewer requirements in the classical languages and included more science. It was a pattern of education followed by many teacher candidates.[31]

In its absorption of the Christian education of the young, this system of elementary and secondary schools blunted the prophetic impact of the church and made it a part of the culture. However, since it was the only system that Lutheran immigrants knew, it continued to influence their attempts to educate their children in the new world.

Christian Education and Lutherans in North America

Colonial Period

The Lutherans who came to the United States did not have a great effect on American society. Lutheran groups were regarded as ethnic enclaves and were viewed with some suspicion by the Anglo-Saxon Protestant majority.

Lutherans did, however, bring with them a great concern for education. The earliest Lutheran colonists were the Swedes who came to Delaware in 1638. These colonists desired to plant and maintain the church, but the Swedish pastors regarded their pastorates as temporary and, after a period of time, the Swedish church withdrew its support. The colonists joined other churches, and Lutheranism faltered in that area. However, one Swedish pastor, John Campanius, translated the *Small Catechism* into the language of the Delaware tribe. It was the first literary document to be translated into one of the native American languages.[32]

The major Lutheran group of the 17th-century colonial period was that of the Germans in Pennsylvania under the leadership of Henry Melchior Muhlenberg. They formed the first Lutheran ministerium and established a system of private Lutheran schools that predated the American public schools by at least 50 years.[33] Like other immigrants, the Pennsylvania Lutherans repeated the patterns from the old country. The family was the central educative agency, and before they went to school children learned much through the worship and instruction of their parents. Many schools were built to aid the education of the children. These schools, the American counterpart of the *Volksschule,* were under the supervision of the pastors, who examined, hired, and supervised the teachers. Not much is known about whether the majority of the teachers were women or men. Through the efforts of parents, pastors, and teachers, children were instructed in the faith. Because of the lack of books and other materials, this was not always easy. The first catechism sponsored by Lutherans in the United States came out in Philadelphia in 1749, and the Ministerium of Pennsylvania produced an Agenda in 1787 that included the Rite of Confirmation. It was a rite heavily influenced by the pietism that also influenced Muhlenberg.[34]

Nineteenth-century immigrants

The Scandinavians who came to the United States in the 19th century adopted a somewhat different pattern of education. Generally speaking, the Swedes and Danes were more ready to embrace the American common schools than were the Norwegians. Unlike many of the Germans, the Swedes supported the public schools as instruments for integration into the language and culture of their new land. Though the Swedes had some parish schools, which usually met in the summer, they regarded those schools as supplementary to the developing public schools.[35] The Swedes depended on their institutions of higher education to conserve the Swedish language and culture for the waves of Swedish immigrants in the 19th century.

The Danes brought with them the tradition of folk schools. Folk schools emphasized great ideas and personalities in history and literature and had no exams, no grades, and no diplomas. The folk schools were not regarded as a substitute for the common schools and tended to emphasize adult education. Faced with the necessity of training pastors for the growing number of Danish congregations, 19th-century Danes turned to the pattern of other immigrant churches—the seminary and preparatory schools.[36] The folk schools disappeared.

The Norwegians made the most concerted effort to establish parochial elementary schools, but by 1870 it was evident that the Norwegian laity supported the American public schools. So beginning in 1870, the Norwegians launched an "academy movement" that resulted in the formation of more than 75 secondary and normal schools.[37] The establishment of the schools witnessed to the enthusiasm of the Norwegian settlers for an education that would equip young people for life in the new land and undergird both their Christian faith and their Norwegian heritage. However, with the increase of public schools in the early 20th century and the Great Depression of the 1930s, the Danish academies disappeared. The surviving schools of the academy movement are the colleges that emerged from the Norwegian tradition.

Meanwhile, by 1820, the German Lutheran schools in Pennsylvania were declining. One factor was certainly the desire of Lutherans to become part of the American mainstream, but another may well have been the shortage of teachers to staff the schools.[38] In any event, Pennsylvania Lutherans disposed of their schools and sent their children to public schools, while placing increasing reliance on the Sunday school for religious education. Thus they adopted the Protestant strategy of public school and Sunday school.

Public schools were a growing phenomenon in the United States in the late 18th and early 19th centuries. Horace Mann, who became superintendent of schools in Massachusetts in 1835, is regarded as the founder of a system of schools that was to serve as the common educating agency for an increasingly diverse population. Because the teachers and curriculum reflected the faith and values of the community, for most Protestants public schools served the purpose of religious education as well. But for specifically religious education the Protestant churches increasingly came to rely on the Sunday school, an institution founded by Robert Raikes in Gloucester, England, in 1780.

Raikes began his school in order to instruct children who worked all week in the factories. It was a school for the poor that taught all the subjects, as well as religion. By 1790 the Sunday school had come to Philadelphia.[39] In the United States the Sunday school became an institution that served all classes of children but restricted its teaching to religion. It was essentially a lay movement and involved many women in its teaching corps. Its function became more and more important as the public schools became more and more secular. And with the secularization of the schools came the realization that the Protestant strategy could not succeed.

In the 19th century Lutherans were influenced not only by American culture but also by rationalistic theology. There was an attempt to Americanize Lutheran theology by accommodating it to rationalist thought and American Protestantism. This reached a zenith with the publication in 1855 of the Definite Synodical Platform by S. S. Schmucker, the first president of Gettysburg Seminary. He attempted to accommodate the Augsburg Confession to the American scene through a liberal and ecumenical revision.

For a time it seemed as if an Americanized Lutheranism might win the day. However, the influx of many confessionally oriented Lutheran immigrants in the mid-19th century weighted the controversy in favor of a confessional Lutheranism. The swing back to a confessional stance was lead by Charles Porterfield Krauth.[40] Thereafter, many Lutherans identified their churches as those of the Unaltered Augsburg Confession.

One of the significant German groups to arrive in the mid-19th century was the group from Saxony led by Martin Stephan. They came to the United States out of resistance to the Prussian Union, a forced union of Lutheran and Reformed churches in their homeland. They also resisted the influence of rationalism and were determined to maintain confessional Lutheran theology in the United States.[41]

When the Saxons came to Missouri in 1839, they began to build schools in order to maintain their faith and culture. They felt they had to educate their children in their own institutions and in their own language in order to preserve the faith. They forged a coalition of home, church, and school that helped children grow up in an environment in which each institution reinforced the other. That nurturing environment served to preserve the community of faith in the midst of an increasingly secular society, but it also led to isolation from it. The potential gospel influence on the structures of society that Luther envisioned was not realized in the 19th and early 20th centuries.

The Lutheran Church–Missouri Synod had and still has many women in the teaching force of its schools. The status of teachers in the Missouri Synod has never been adequately clarified. Male teachers have chafed under the yoke of their second-class status, but the women have had an even heavier burden. While male teachers have received calls to their teaching ministries, the women have been given only nontenured contracts.[42] However, the LCMS is not alone in needing to deal honestly with the contributions and status of women in the educational ministry of the church. Lay women, teachers, and deaconesses have played significant roles in the Christian education enterprise of all Lutheran churches.

Twentieth century

In the 20th century, Lutheran Christian education in day schools is concentrated in the LCMS. It has a professional society for teachers in day schools and other educational agencies of the church, the Lutheran Education Association. The Wisconsin Evangelical Lutheran Synod also has a number of elementary and high schools. The American Lutheran Church and Lutheran Church in America have a significantly smaller number of schools, many of them preschools. Their professional organization is the American Lutheran Education Association.

All the major Lutheran church bodies produce curriculum materials for use in the Sunday school and other agencies of Christian education in the church. The content of those materials was not much affected by the theological and educational currents of mainstream Protestantism in the early part of the 20th century.

Nineteenth-century liberal theological thought and early 20th-century educational thought came together in the formation of the Religious Education Association in 1903. The emphasis on liberal theology and developmental psychology continued until the impact of Karl Barth's neoorthodox theology after World War II. That caused a swing back to a more biblically based revelational theology. It is significant that post-World War II literature referred to education in the church as Christian education rather than religious education.[43]

Now, in the 1980s, there appears to be a swing back to the importance of developmental psychology and its relevance for Lutheran educational materials. This development is in tension with another trend, which calls for a focus on biblical material.

Lutheran curriculum materials in the latter part of the 20th century incorporated prevailing educational theory. There was careful attention to educational objectives, both in general and for each age level. Materials were designed that reflected the developmental level of the learners for whom they were intended. The relation of the Christian faith to issues in Christian living was emphasized, and local congregations and teachers were given much responsibility in determining how the curriculum would be shaped.

Historical and Theological Implications for Christian Education in Lutheran Churches

The Jewish and early Christian experience shows the importance of the family working within the faith community in a thorough education of both children and adults. The Jewish family was the primary agency of education, with the synagogue as an additional aid at a later time. Then came the schools that originated with the synagogues. The family, synagogue, and school formed a coalition that passed on and preserved the faith of a religious community that has survived countless dispersions and difficulties.

In early Christianity it was also the family and the faith community that were the primary agencies of education. Within the faith community there gradually evolved an extensive and thorough system of education for those seeking to be baptized into the Christian faith. When the closeness and intensity of that educational process broke down as Christianity became the religion of the state, the Christian faith became an established religion that lost much of its power to change the society. The experience of the Jewish and Christian faith communities again points out the enormous importance of the family, in league with the church, as the primary agencies of education in the faith. However, it also illustrates a continuing tension for all faith communities—the tension between isolation from the surrounding culture and absorption by it.

Luther wanted the Christians of his day to have a worldview that held all of life together. He wanted Christians to understand that they were members of both the kingdom of Christ and the kingdom of the world. Both were God's kingdoms. Christians, called by the gospel into the community of faith, were to carry out their calling in the common places of everyday life. They were to be messengers of God's judgment and grace in serving their fellow human beings. Luther hoped that families would educate their children into this worldview. He even produced the catechisms as a help. However, he saw that families could not do the job alone, so he appealed to public officeholders to build and maintain schools that would train Christians in the skills necessary for carrying out their calling. He could make such an appeal because the public sector was an extension of the church and family and any school maintained by the state would reinforce the same worldview. Although Luther's proposals did not have much immediate impact on public schooling, the European public schools that later developed incorporated and reinforced the common religion. However, that development again made Christianity a diffuse civil religion that lost much of its prophetic and transforming power.

Aside from contributions to the educational systems of his day, Luther made a contribution to the process of learning in Christian education through the struggles with God that resulted in his Reformation theology. Luther struggled to find a gracious God, but experienced God only as judge. Through his work as a biblical professor he came to the insight that the God who *demands* is the God who *gives* what is demanded. The gospel offers the gift, which faith receives. That new insight, and all that it meant for his theology, took Luther a lifetime to interpret.

There is a cue here for learning in Lutheran churches. It is learning that begins with struggle over life's issues, experiences new insights into the meaning of the gospel for living with those issues, and interprets those new understandings to others.[44]

There is also a cue here for the content of education in Lutheran churches. The content is not only biblical and theological, but also the life-and-death issues of human existence. Learning that results in significant new insights about the meaning of the gospel begins with the personal and social issues that reveal death in the midst of life and moves to insights of the gospel's life in the midst of death. Lutheran theology is dialectical, and Lutheran education should be also. It should deal with death and life, law and gospel, sinners and saints, and all the other ambiguities of life.[45] To do less is to settle for a conventional faith and a conventional church that offers no prophetic challenge to confront people and the social structures and bring a message of hope that is able to transform individuals and society.[46]

When Lutherans came to America, they (especially those in Pennsylvania) tried to recapture the cohesive nature of mutually reinforcing agencies by building schools to help the family and the church in the task of education. However, the social forces of America won out, and early Lutherans opted for the Protestant strategy of public schools and Sunday schools. That strategy worked as long as the public schools were, in effect, Protestant schools. But as they became increasingly secular, it also became increasingly apparent that the Protestant strategy had failed. The public schools cannot teach the faith that enables Christians to know their calling and be equipped to carry it out in the world.

The Challenge for Lutheran Education

The Lutheran Church looks to the future with new challenges. The first task is to strengthen families so that they educate their children in the Christian faith in such an all-pervasive manner that the children never know themselves to be other than Christian.[47]

However, families cannot do the job alone in a pluralistic society in which many worldviews exist side by side and children are exposed to them in various ways. The church must also work at being a nurturing community that uses Word and sacrament to nurture its members and strengthen them in their primary calling of faith so that they are equipped to carry out their calling in the world. This means that the church must continually seek out the most useful educational strategies for the task.

TWO

FOUNDATIONS FOR CHRISTIAN EDUCATION

Eugene C. Kreider

On the way to the villages of Caesarea Philippi, Jesus asked his disciples who people said that he was. The disciples gave several answers: "John the Baptist." "Elijah." "One of the prophets." Then Jesus asked the disciples, "But who do you say that I am?" Peter answered, "You are the Christ" (Mark 8:27-30).

This account of Peter's confession is simple and direct. Jesus' presence among the people did not make his identity self-evident. Rather, it elicited a variety of responses, including Peter's. And that's the way it has been ever since.

The Christ whom the church has confessed as Lord and taught about from generation to generation is one who is always known in experiences that combine his presence and the human perception of who he is. The work of Christian education is to tell about those experiences of Christ and people in the past and to encourage similar experiences in the present. It is a way of helping people perceive the grace of God in Jesus and make sense out of that experience for their own lives.

The Dialog of Faith and the Way to Foundations

Christian education is a living experience in that it is an experience that affects the way life is lived. It involves one's understanding of the realities of faith and the ways one responds to these realities out of transforming convictions and commitments. Moreover, Christian education embraces the uses one makes of those convictions and commitments in the ongoing involvements that characterize life in the human community.

This claim for Christian education has its origin and warrant in the confession of Jesus through the ages by the Christian community. That confession is a dialogical experience, an experience that is informed by the reality of Christ and by the faith of believers. Such an experience is the starting point for speaking about the foundations for Christian education.

Because of the dialog that takes place in Christian education between the reality of Christ and the faith of believers, one cannot speak of foundations for Christian education directly and immediately, as though they were discrete, self-authenticating, and universally applicable bodies of knowledge capable of being used in the educational setting as ingredients are used in a recipe, generally effective in and of themselves, though carefully measured and sequenced. Such discrete bodies of knowledge are the disciplines of study that stand behind and give rise to educational foundations.

Foundations for Christian education, then, are the results of reflective interaction with specific disciplines of study, challenging them with one's assumptions and being challenged by the information and meanings they set forth. Foundations are the conclusions one reaches about the way any given material from the disciplines of study can be used in the teaching/learning environment.

In what follows we shall speak about the Bible, theology, and the social sciences as the disciplines of study that are sources of the specific foundations for Christian education, namely, the biblical witness, theological reflection, and the contextual realities of the educational setting. These foundations provide the materials for organizing the work of Christian education around certain principles and for developing the objectives, purposes, and goals to be achieved through learning designs and teaching methods in the educational setting.

Disciplines of Study

The Bible, theology, and the contemporary social sciences are the disciplines of study standing behind the work of Christian education.

The Bible

The Bible is the Holy Scripture of the Christian faith. As such it is a record of God's revelation to the ancient people Israel and to the later generations of Christians. That revelation is specific, linked to historical circumstances and times. It is God's Word to humankind through particular individuals and events. That particularity is always part of the meaning of revelation in the Bible.

The Bible tells us that God does not come to creation with full self-disclosure. Revelation partakes of paradox. God comes, to be sure, to make God's will and way known. In this knowing one encounters God. But God always "hides" in the specific vehicles through which God "reveals." As God's revelation, the Bible is therefore both a testimony to the way God comes into relationship with the world and the account of God's purpose in coming into relationship. God comes to reveal the divine will for human life.

That divine will is expressed in different ways in different times and places. Thus we cannot view the Bible as a record of simple repetition, with God saying and doing the same things over and over again from generation to generation. Though sameness might be claimed for revelation on the basis of the sameness we see in the created world, revelation bears the characteristics of the events and persons through which it becomes known.

By the same token, we cannot assert that revelation is so particular that it is uniquely contained by and for the person or circumstance for which it is meant. Revelation occurs in history, and finds thereby a point of contact in what is available to people in history in general. Availability means that people other than the one or ones for whom revelation was originally intended can know and learn from such revelation, even though limited to their own particularity and, therefore, to their own perception of the revelation.

Thus when we view the Bible as a discipline of study, informing the biblical witness, which becomes a foundation for Christian education, we are concerned primarily with understanding the Bible as revelation that is always particular but not exclusive. This means that when we use the Bible in Christian education, we cannot assume that its revelation is either all of one kind or exclusively particular and therefore meaningless in the history of salvation. The Bible as revelation points us to the ongoing activity of God with humankind, which, indeed, is the history of salvation.

God continues to be revealed to each one and all, to the end that God's will shall be done. So Christian education continues to study that record of revelation, claimed by the Christian community as Holy Scripture, in order to learn anew from God and teach God's will to others.

Theology

Etymologically, theology is the study of or discourse about God. In the Christian community, theology is the study of or discourse about the God we know through the revelation of Scripture and through the community's use of that revelation in its ongoing life. Thus theology, broadly speaking, includes the study of the events and teachings of the Christian community through the history of the church and in the contemporary experiences of Christian beliefs in everyday life. As such, theology includes Christian history and ethics.

As a discipline of study, theology has a specific focus. It is not random discourse, but the rational and systematic way one makes sense out of the confession of God. Christian theology is therefore the way the Christian community makes sense out of Jesus the Christ.

Theology as the study of or discourse about God produces a heritage of experiences, ideas, and insights that have become part of the ongoing tradition of the Christian community. Gathering up what has been and is known about God, this heritage is in one sense a rational and verbal heritage. Making sense out of the confession of God relies heavily on ordered thinking and the logic of reasoning. And one might argue that, because language is a primary vehicle of the discourse, theology's chief ingredient is verbal expression. When we think of theology, certainly books, other writings, as well as discussions and conversations come to mind. In large measure, theology is the use of the human cognitive capacity to apprehend God, as far as that capacity will allow, and to express that apprehension in words.

And yet theology is more than language that serves to express the logic of reasoning about God. Discourse about God encompasses the whole of the human capacity to apprehend and understand God. This means that as theology speaks about God, it uses the awareness that comes also from the affective and volitional sides of human nature. God is known not only in the head, but also in the heart and will.

Theology that grows out of biblical revelation must give attention to the interrelationship of the language of head, heart, and will. God is known in the heights and depths of life that even the best of head language cannot comprehend. God is also known through images and the imagination that spring from feelings and desires that often know no words. Discourse about God, therefore, must find forms of human expression to capture the nuances of the whole of life, and through those human nuances experience the nuances of God. Though finally God is the ultimate mystery, God is perhaps best apprehended through the language of metaphor, as in, "A mighty fortress is our God."

As Christian education uses the discipline of theology in its work, it must center on the reflective capacity of theology to gather up experiences, ideas, and insights about God and the world and make sense out of them for human existence and for life in the human community. In Christian education, theology does not exist for itself. It is a discipline that informs the life we live under God by providing structures for thinking, feeling, and acting in respect to what is known about God in the community of faith in past and present.

Thus, Christian education needs to take the heritage of theology seriously, perhaps more seriously than it has in some periods of its past, because theology gives our head, heart, and will language about God, and it gives the meanings contained in that interrelationship of those languages an order and significance for contemporary life. That order and significance are more than artifacts or historical data. Together they provide criteria for linking life to the faithful in the Christian community in the past and for living life as meaningfully as possible in the present, with hope in the age to come.

Contemporary social sciences

The social sciences provide psychological and sociological data from contemporary life that help to describe the human condition to which the gospel is addressed. These data are not religious or theological in orientation, but the insights and conclusions drawn from such data make valuable contributions to the religious and theological concerns of the Christian community.

The psychological and sociological data most helpful to Christian education have to do with human development and with the social and emotional growth of people. In order for Christian education to do its work effectively and achieve its purpose in assisting persons to perceive, respond to, and participate in God's continuing activity and revelation, educators must consider carefully and thoughtfully what the social sciences have taught us about the abilities and learning readiness of people at various ages and stages of life. Drawing on biological and psychological data about growth and maturation, studies in human development have told us much not only about how people learn, but also about how we should teach in order to make the learning experiences appropriate for the learner. Teaching is not just a matter of erasing ignorance by filling that void with knowledge, and some teaching does not distinguish carefully enough between what the teacher knows and what the learner *can* know or *needs to* know.

In addition to a concern for the human development of learners from the perspective of overall physical and mental growth, Christian education must pay equal attention to the learners' emotional and social development. Too often the environment where Christian education takes place in the congregation—the Sunday school, the confirmation class, youth-ministry events, an adult forum, and other structured classroom settings in which both children and adults are taught—does not give adequate attention to the way learners feel about themselves or their associates, or to the learners' ability to interact with others in a constructive way. The skills needed for constructive social behavior are not genetically acquired. The values they presuppose are not culturally innate either. Both need to be taught and learned. And the more aware that Christian educators are about these factors, the more positive and fulfilling will be the growth experiences of individuals in the community of faith.

Most curriculum materials and the supplements for teachers that go with them incorporate the insights of developmental studies in such aids as age-level characteristics, charts, and handbooks, and they suggest how to use these insights in the learning environment. Above all, data from the social sciences remind teachers not to go too fast too soon with what is taught or expected of learners. The teacher's greatest challenge is to know and respect the learner's human capacities and readiness to learn as part of the "giveness" of creation, making the learning experience fit for the gospel.

Integration of the discipline

Each of the three disciplines of study has a distinct contribution to make to Christian education, yet each informs the others. The Bible is the record of God's revelation to a covenant people. That revelation is always known in the context of history, but it is never simply to be equated with history. Similarly, theology grows out of the biblical materials, but it carries forward the story of those materials into new times wherein different life contexts demand fresh interpretations of the age-old story of faith. The same is true of the social sciences and the contextual situations they address. The insights of the social sciences help us know and understand individuals and the human community better. In doing so, they can help us teach and learn the message of the Bible and the tradition of faith effectively. But social sciences cannot provide the criteria for understanding or evaluating the character of faith and life in the past.

A Living Tradition:
The Question of Interpretation

Christian education is a teaching/learning process through which the tradition of faith and life from the past is made available to those in the present so that they might claim the faith for themselves and assist those of the next generation to receive it as theirs. But the movement from past to present to future is not a simple, linear process in which the formulations of belief are passed on intact and unchanged, as the baton in a relay race is passed on from one runner to the next, remaining the same throughout the race, though carried in different hands. This movement is a complex, life-imbued movement in which the tradition of faith always bears the marks of those who live it.

Therefore the tradition of faith received from the past must always be interpreted in the course of making it known in the present. One needs to discover what the questions of life were in the past and what meaning the Christian faith gave people then for answering those questions. One needs to find out, as far as possible, how our foreparents made sense out of the faith for their lives. This means it is imperative to recover the living tradition from the disciplines of study in order to determine the educational foundations that will provide a meaningful experience of faith today. When this is done adequately, one can begin to grasp the significance of faith for daily life and appreciate the way the biblical promises of salvation can be relevant for life in the present.

The work of interpretation, the hermeneutical task, is at least two-fold. First, it involves examining the disciplines of study that bear the tradition to us by methods appropriate to their subject matter in order to minimize prejudice and false assumptions. The Bible needs to be studied with the tools of biblical scholarship and its message conveyed out of the results of that scholarship. Theology, likewise, must be subject to its own methods in order that the clarity it can bring to faith might be realized. The same is true of the social sciences. They must be studied in terms of their own methods of inquiry, analysis, and interpretation.

Second, the work of interpretation involves raising questions with the tradition out of one's own cultural setting and listening to the critical questions from the past that come to challenge and encourage the way the life of faith is formulated today. Our foreparents understood life under God in a certain way and lived accordingly. But we cannot conclude that knowing the past and living it the same way in the present is the goal of Christian education. On the other hand, the faith we live today is not unrelated to the past, and we need to test our expressions of faith and life with the experiences of the historic Christian community of which we are a part.

Moreover, we need to take the results of interpretative efforts and decide how they will be used in educational programs. There is another set of questions we ask out of our present situation. For example, will our concern be with what was believed and confessed in the community of faith through the ages? If so, then our programs will concentrate on the content of faith and the formulations of beliefs. Or will our concern be with how we can be Christians together as we live the faith? If that is the case, then the shape of education will be determined by the way Christian beliefs are expressed in the lives of individuals in community.

These latter questions, like the disciplines of study themselves, are not mutually exclusive. Each has a bearing on the other and complements the other. They do, however, represent natural emphases embodying assumptions and tendencies that ultimately determine the way one views the biblical witness, theological reflection, and the contextual realities as the foundations for planned learning experiences.

Christian Education Foundations

Biblical witness

Biblical witness is the first foundation. This witness is the story of God's relationship with people from creation through the history of a particular people in the Old and New Testaments, sustained to the end of the age by the hope of salvation in the promise of God.

The biblical story is not just a story *about* people, to be told as a tale from history; it is a story *of* people. In its telling and retelling God is present again, and its hearers are called on to claim the story as their own. As such, the biblical story is an incarnational form of revelation. It bears God and the divine will to people.

The relationship of God with people begins with a covenant initiated by God and responded to by people to whom God comes in word and deed, marking forever a relationship that is indissoluble. That relationship can be broken by sin, but it is never destroyed. God's word and deed, which together are the basis for covenant, are vividly demonstrated in the story of God's people in the Hebrew Scriptures and supremely manifested in Jesus of Nazareth. The story of God with people is the story of the reign of God in the world, the ongoing presence of God that creates and redeems in order that God's kingdom might come and God's will be done.

Christian education needs to help people know the details of the biblical story of salvation and it needs to nurture the unfolding of that story in people's lives so that they might walk in God's way. The experience of walking in God's way leads to the experience of wholeness. As the story is taught and learned, it is remembered as the possession of a people. And in that remembering, the community of faith is formed.

Theological reflection

Theological reflection is the second foundation for Christian education. It is the way we organize our knowledge about God and make it meaningful for us. Once again it is bringing together the God we know in the Bible and in the experiences of daily life. From these two sources we derive what we teach about God.

The God of covenant is a God who wants to be known in God's will for creation. Such a God reaches out to be immanent in creation, as well as transcendent over it, in word and deed. Actually the *word* and *deed* of God are understood to be one and the same. Both of these words are translated from the same Hebrew word. God's word and deed is known in different ways at different times, through patriarchs, prophets, and kings, as well as through ordinary folk and the events of history. In Jesus of Nazareth God was incarnate; the word and deed of God became flesh.

As God reaches out, so God provides for human response in word and deed. We teach people to follow God's way, to live as creatures of the creator, doing God's will. That will has been variously understood through history, but in all understandings, it calls for love and justice in the human community. God seeks the wholeness, the *shalom,* of creation. God's way for us to walk is the way toward wholeness. This we do through prayer and through acts of love and justice.

Theological reflection also tells us that the way toward wholeness is marked by sin and brokenness: "I can will what is right, but I cannot do it. For I do not do the good I want, but the evil I do not want is what I do. Now if I do what I do´not want, it is no longer I that do it, but sin which dwells within me" (Rom. 7:18b-20). In the face of that condition we do not teach despair in ourselves or rejection by God. God is a loving and forgiving God, whose whole action in respect to the world is grace. God reaches out to creation to forgive and reconcile all things. That is the message of the cross of Christ. In the death of Christ, who bore the punishment for sin, God accepts us as we are and asks us to do the same for ourselves and others.

Theological reflection is a way of speaking about the guidance of God's Spirit. We are not trying to manage God, but are rather allowing God to manage us. Nevertheless, we must recognize that it is the process of our own reflection that prevents us from surrendering all to God. So, we can speak of theological reflection as that which judges or provides a norm for experience, and experience as that which judges or provides a norm for theological reflection.

Contextual realities

Contextual realities comprise the third foundation for Christian education. These realities include decisions on the theoretical information about how people learn and how that information will be used in teaching, if used at all. These realities include the selection and availability of curriculum materials and the training of teachers who will use those materials. They involve the learners and all that each learner brings to the learning setting, those shaping influences that have molded one's life in the past, and the present experiences through which one grows day after day.

Contextual realities are the framework of relationships between teacher, learner, and what is to be learned, as these relationships are made possible through the physical and emotional environments of the learning setting. Teachers need to know as much about themselves as they can. They need to know their students in and out of the learning setting and help the students know each other that way. They need to be clear and confident about the objectives and goals for learning and about the methods to be used toward those ends. The skill of teaching is to know when the student needs the teacher (to give information, to motivate, to challenge and encourage), and when to leave the student alone to learn. In Christian education a teacher is, above all, a resource for someone else's journey in faith.

Every learning setting is different, just as every congregation is different. It is not possible, therefore, to prescribe precisely how the teaching/learning process will go in each place. But it is important for all involved in education to be aware of the personal and congregational factors that come together to create the climate for teaching and learning. One way to bring about this awareness is to make some assessment of the needs and resources of the congregation and bring those together with the congregation's mission statement.

Behind each congregational Christian education program are systems of support and hindrance. Those systems are both external and internal to the educational program. Those responsible for education must find ways of using the strengths of the external support systems, in the form of interested people and other available resources. Those responsible for education must also shore up internal weaknesses and assemble the internal strengths, particularly in personal commitments, attitudes, and enthusiasm. These internal strengths can be used to diffuse whatever opposition may come from external hindrances.

As foundations, biblical witness, theological reflection, and contextual realities are the means by which Christian educators attend to the tradition of faith and bring it to contemporary expression to touch and mold the lives of others.

Organizing Principles for Teaching and Learning

The organizing principles for education are the personal insights, attitudes, and assumptions that determine how the teaching/learning environment will be structured and how the materials derived from the foundations will be used. At times such principles are in the forefront of one's consciousness and highly visible in the planning process. At other times they are like unconscious forces buried deep below the surface but with driving, insistent power capable of determining how things will work on the surface. Organizing principles may be mere prejudices that have their origin in personal preferences and predilections, without much attention given to the foundations recognized by the community, as would be the case for someone teaching the Bible solely out of a personal reading of it. Such principles may also take into account the way the biblical, theological, and contextual foundations influence insights, attitudes, and assumptions. In any case, those principles are the filters through which educational material is perceived and used.

It is important, therefore, to emphasize that the organizing principles are not the foundations themselves, because people sometimes speak and work as though they were. In a discussion among teachers, for example, one might hear that a lesson should be organized around the biblical witness or some theological reflection or a contextual reality. Those foundations do, in fact, provide the materials for the lesson, but they do not teach themselves nor do they have a value for teaching and learning independent of what teachers think about them. We get into problems when we assume that foundational materials are the organizing principles, because we unwittingly create a false objectification of the content and process of learning or the illusion that organizing principles are formally external and can be applied as independent arbiters and guides wherever necessary.

The organizing principles carry forward the questions of interpretation discussed above, especially those fundamental questions about how the living tradition will be used with learners. That is why it is so important for teachers to begin their planning with questions they ask themselves about their own personal understanding of things and with questions they have about the meaning of faith gathered up in the tradition.

Teachers need to know who they are and why they teach what they do. That self-knowledge will make it easier for them to engage the lesson personally and to model a conviction and commitment for their students. This self-knowledge does not have to be deep introspection or long, probing inquiries. It is best and most easily achieved in those teacher conversations at the lesson-planning level, when conscious effort is put forth to help each other get at personal "agendas." Those personal "agendas" are the factors that will determine how the materials to be taught will be organized and used in the learning setting.

Central Objectives and Goals
for Christian Education

A central objective for Christian education is a comprehensive statement of the overall purposes of education that is applicable to all groups within a given community of faith. It is a general statement of what education should be about and serves as the basis for educational designs, from denominational curriculum building to the setting of objectives and goals for individual learning sessions.

Because it is general in nature, an educational objective needs to be translated into specific goals that state precisely what is to be achieved in the learning session and that, therefore, can be evaluated afterward. Thus the central objective for Christian education provides the broad framework for the specific tasks that need to be undertaken and completed for and in the learning experience.

An example of a central educational objective is one that has been used by the American Lutheran Church and the Lutheran Church in America in the last two decades: "to assist persons to perceive, respond to, and participate in God's continuing activity and revelation, particularly in Jesus Christ, in the human and Christian communities as they deal with their continual life involvements of being a person, relating to persons and groups, and living in society, culture, and the physical universe."

This central objective contains the three basic types of objectives and goals for all Christian education: *thinking, feeling,* and *acting.* It is the purpose of education to bring about changes in people's lives, evidenced in the way they act, by a change in attitudes and feelings on the basis of increased knowledge and understanding. Applied to Christian education, this purpose means that education within the Christian community should bring about increased knowledge of God's activity in the world and new ways to respond to that activity through life involvements with self, others, and the broader environments of society and world.

Preparing central objectives

The best way for Christian educators to understand central objectives is for them to write their own. After they come to some decision about what the Bible, theology, and the contemporary context say is the content and process of education, let them be challenged to formulate their own general statement of purposes that involves the learner in new thinking, feeling, and acting about God's way with creation through the experiences of the Christian community.

Then let them take the next step and explore how their central objective can be translated into the three types of objectives and goals for the students in their learning settings. In this process, point out several things. First, though the thinking, feeling, and acting objectives for the learning session are stated generally, the corresponding goals must be very specific, leaving no question about the learning task and its desired outcomes. Second, help them to realize that as they formulate the objectives and goals for their class, these should be stated in terms of the desired outcomes in the learner. This point may seem superfluous, but in actual practice, it is often what the teacher does in the learning process that appears to be more important. Care must be taken, therefore, that objectives and goals are learner-oriented.

Language is crucial in maintaining learner-orientation in the planning. Whether one uses infinitives (to know, to feel, to act) or gerunds (knowing, feeling, acting) or subject-predicate statements (the learner will know, feel, act), it must be clear that the teacher's involvement in the learning experience is for the sake of the learner. Especially if infinitives and gerunds are used, it must be made clear what the subjects and objects of those verbal forms are. For example, in the central objective for Christian education stated above, it is clear, even without the specificity of a goal statement, that the infinitives "to perceive, respond to, and participate in" refer to the "persons" mentioned just before and that these experiences are definitely oriented toward the learner who is *assisted* in the experiences.

Types of objectives and goals

Objectives and goals can be stated in a variety of ways. The following objectives, along with their accompanying goals, can be used effectively in planning the learning experiences: instructional objectives and goals, process content objectives and goals, and product content objectives and goals. Each focuses on a different aspect of the teaching/ learning process. Yet all aim at change in the learner.

Instructional objectives have to do with the subject matter, the context of instruction. They describe what the learners will learn and the experiences they will have in the process of the learning. Such objectives are stated in terms of perceived learner needs and the course of study aimed at meeting those needs. Formally, they come closest to being teacher-oriented, especially when the infinitive is used in stating the objectives. An example of such an objective for the study of Mark's gospel is: "to study the historical and geographical background of Mark's gospel." A goal for this objective might be: "to provide information for students to learn about five geographical places in Mark's gospel where Jesus' ministry occurred."

Process content objectives describe what is to be achieved during the course of the learning experience. They do not presuppose a particular outcome for the total experience, but identify the activity aimed at in the flow of the experience. Nevertheless, because they are stated in terms of process, they assume that the experience learners have along the way has intention and points to some conclusion. They are not open-ended objectives but objectives that are means toward some culminating experience. An example of such an objective for a study of Mark's gospel is: "Members of the class shall reflect on the meaning of the parables in Mark 4 for their lives." A goal for this objective might be: "Each student shall share with two other students some personal reactions to one of the parables in this chapter of Mark."

Product content objectives describe concretely the action on the part of the learner that is indicative of the knowledge gained through the learning experience. These objectives, sometimes called behavioral objectives, define the particular outcome or end of the learning experience. The change or growth in the learner is the result of the influence of all the components in the learning process. Product content objectives are sometimes difficult to evaluate, especially if the desired outcome in the learner can be expressed only at a future time beyond the immediate learning experience. And yet, that does not always have to be the case. An example of a product content objective that could be evaluated at the end of an immediate learning experience involving a study of Mark's gospel is: "Members of the class shall study the teachings of Jesus in Mark's gospel." A goal for this objective might be: "Members of the class shall report to the class what Jesus said in his parables about God's relationship to people."

Evaluating the learning process

Objectives and goals are ways the purposes of education are achieved. They determine not only the desired outcomes in the learner but also the program components of the learning process, and, together with these components, are the basis for evaluating the learning process. Measurability of objectives and goals depends on their specificity, especially in the case of goals, which are the specific ways objectives are achieved. The more specific the goal, the easier it is to measure what happened in the learning experience.

Evaluation of a learning experience involves testing the efficiency of the program components in meeting the goals of learning, and the effectiveness of the goals in achieving the objectives. For example, in evaluating the product content objective above, one would ask if the activities in the learning experience did make a study of Jesus' teachings in Mark possible and in such a way that the students could report about what the parables say about God's relationship to people.

Foundations for Christian education are the biblical, theological, and contextual data for an organic model of teaching and learning within a living community. They are the basis for the design and execution of the learning experience.

THREE

THE LEARNING COMMUNITY

Jean Bozeman

Learning is like breathing—as long as we are alive, it is basic to our very existence. We can breathe pure or polluted air, we can breathe in short gasps or with long, smooth breaths—or we can cease to breathe, and die. Likewise, we can interact with and learn from our environment, or we can passively accept the forces that surround us. However, all of these involve learning at some level, unless we are unconscious or nonfunctional. Some years ago a parish educational theme stated it this way: "As long as you live you learn; as long as you learn you live." If learning is a constant in our lives, then the question becomes not, Should we learn? but rather, What is the nature and style of the learning we value, deprecate, stimulate, or ignore?

The church learns as it lives and grows. In fact, learning is at the very heart of the church's life and mission.

The whole church teaches and the whole church learns; this confirms that every part of the life and work of a congregation has educational effects—good or bad. The church teaches and learns in the way the members of the congregation think, the language they use, the attitudes they reveal, the values they uphold, the way they treat and relate to other people and one another. Everything the church is and does reveals concepts of God and Christ, its understanding of the nature and mission of the church and Christian community. The church's understandings of itself and its relationship to the universe, the earth, and humankind everywhere have educational impact.[1]

In Deuteronomy 6:4-9 we have perhaps our earliest explicit model of a learning community:

OBJECTIVE:	Hear, O Israel: The Lord our God is one Lord. You shall love the Lord your God.
NATURE:	With all your heart, and with all your soul, and with all your might.
PARTICIPANTS:	You, your children and your neighbors
CONTENT:	When you sit in your house, and when you walk by the way, and when you lie down and when you rise
METHODS:	Diligent teaching (intentional) Talking (formal and informal conversation) Binding as a sign Writing/displaying

Our task in this chapter will be to use the Deuteronomic model to describe characteristics of the congregation as a learning community. Even though the structure may vary, depending on size, location, current events, and gifts of the people, there are universal aspects to all these communities we call the church.

Objective of the Learning Community

"Hear, O Israel: The Lord our God is one Lord, and you shall love the Lord your God. . . ."

As we read in Deuteronomy 6, the announcement for Israel was direct and clearly stated. Whatever else might follow for this nation, the hearers knew that the oneness of God as Lord and their relationship to God would be the central focus for all of life.

Too often we leap into developing programs, classes, and schools with the assumption that everyone knows the objectives, when in actuality the objectives may be as varied as the number of persons present.

Leaders, too, express varied objectives as they invite participation based on tradition, obligation, friendship, or need for knowledge.

First and foremost, we must state that the purpose of the learning community is not education per se. Our objective will be no less than that which the gospel writer laid out for Jesus' ministry—to understand for ourselves and to share with others the news, "The time is fulfilled, and the kingdom of God is at hand; repent, and believe in the gospel" (Mark 1:15). Jesus preached the good news and the values of the kingdom, which becomes our gift and symbol of God's active presence uniting the past, present, and future of our lives. We also have the privilege of standing on the other side of the cross and hearing our objective further stated this way:

> Go therefore and make disciples of all nations, baptizing them in the name of the Father and of the Son and of the Holy Spirit, teaching them to observe all that I have commanded you; and lo, I am with you always, to the close of the age (Matt. 28:19-20).

That gospel message is the foundation of the church's teaching, identity, focus, and mission as we are invited to be the new creation. The urgency and content of our objective needs to be kept foremost as it shapes the communicator, the process, structure, and settings for the learning task of the church.

> Christian theology is based on the unique event Jesus the Christ, and in spite of the infinite meaning of this event it remains this event and, as such, the criterion of every religious experience. This event is given to experience and not derived from it. Therefore, experience receives and does not produce. . . . Two extremes must be avoided in this procedure: the influence of the medium, the experience of the theologian, should not be so small that the result is a repetition instead of a transformation, and it should not be so large that the result is a new production instead of a transformation.[2]

As soon as we are clear about the objective, we hasten to state that to carry out that objective—to be the new creation—we will see the gathered people as teaching/learning communities. The church is called to teach, just as it is to worship, or it will not be the church. Teaching is at the very heart of who we are and to whom we belong.

The Nature of the Learning Community: Spirit and Image

". . . with all your heart, and with all your soul, and with all your might."

We have all heard and perhaps used the phrase, "spittin' image," meaning that someone looks just like another person. In a sermon to our seminary community, Walter Wangerin Jr., pastor and author, showed us a deeper meaning for that phrase. He recalled his relationship with his beloved grandfather and the proud, but confused feelings he experienced as he heard folks say, "He's the spittin' image of his grandpa." He wondered, was it looks, his grandpa's tobacco chewing and accurate "spitter style," voice, or walk, that made him the spittin' image of his grandpa? Later he learned that this phrase had its roots in the southern part of the United States, where the drawled "spittin' image" came from the original phrase, "spirit and image."

Fascinated with this concept, I asked my mother, who grew up in North Carolina, what she knew about the phrase. She recalled it used this way: "She is so much like you that she must have been spit out of your mouth." That is how the folks were describing Pastor Wangerin and his grandfather. Physical characteristics and mannerisms were a part of this image, but even deeper was the sense that their way of thinking, their heart and soul, and their very being were one with another. He must have been spit out of his grandpa's mouth.

This is what the writer of Deuteronomy 6:5 was trying to express in using the words, "with all your heart, and with all your soul, and with all your might." That is also the description of our learning community—in the spittin' image of God who has and is creating, redeeming, and sanctifying us each day. As such, this community will see itself as disciples who bring their total life to the community and the world. These people will be a community of story and belonging who live an intentional life toward decision, transformation, and action.

They will be a community of hope, joy, and new life. This community could describe itself with these characteristics:

1. The community appreciates and incorporates the fullness of each person's life within the community. As the people of God come with their heart, mind, and soul, they bring their intellect, emotions, feelings, conflicts, joys, and daily tasks to the community.

2. Belonging and kinship are symbols, as well as lifegiving reality, as the concepts "children of God," "brothers and sisters in Christ," and "family of God" become the very heart, mind, and soul of this community.

3. The community sees itself as disciples who accept the gift of the kingdom as well as the responsibilities of servanthood; they are no longer volunteers. As disciples, there is the responsibility and challenge to be knowledgeable in the Word, to be a servant, to follow, continually to be the child of faith, to enter a life of prayer and devotion and out of this life-style to share the gospel.

4. It is a community with a past, present, and future. The heart, mind, and soul has a memory, for without our story we have no ties to our past and wander aimlessly in the wilderness. Our story gives us the gift of community and moves us beyond individualism. With our heart, mind, and soul we interpret this story in the present. For we are chosen people who believe that this is our given moment in history to witness to the Word of God. In light of this past and present, the community sees itself as a community "on the way," because it is the new creation and, at the same time, it has a vision of the "not yet" of the new creation.

5. It is a community that learns by doing and intentionally reflecting on its life. The ethical issues of work and play, the joys and crises of our personal lives, the care of our world, and our personal and corporate acts of service will be the immediate agenda for biblical and theological study and reflection. In other instances, the environment and relations of the community will prepare and teach the foundations for later articulation.

At a recent family reunion, my young cousins met new relatives, fumbled with concepts of aunt, uncle, cousin, and at the end of a lively day, exchanged hugs and words of "I love you" and "See you soon."

In this way children were developing their understanding of security, trust, and belonging long before they could intellectualize about these concepts and experiences. As the community incorporates and experiences itself as the faith community, it becomes the place to experience and express this as God's event.

6. It becomes a community of decision and transformation as we open our hearts, minds, and souls to the action of the Spirit in our learning, doing, reflecting, and acting.

> Although our faith is more likely to become rusty from lack of use than to be swept away by crises and change, it does change as contemporary contexts change. That is, our understanding of God's love in our life changes as we are changed by our life experiences. The gift of faith does not change, but the way we live out our new relationship with God in Jesus Christ is a continued story.[3]

7. It is a community of joy and excitement. The gospel is good news and lifts one's heart, mind, and soul to heights of merriment and ecstasy.

Participants in the Learning Community

"You, your children, your neighbor."

The Deuteronomic writer was clear in stating that the central proclamation that is accepted with all one's heart, mind, and soul is for our children, our neighbors, and ourselves. In the teaching/learning process we are inclined to become immediately concerned with what is imparted to others; however, through this text we are reminded that we first hear and love, and that out of this relationship we in turn impart the Word to others. The Word becomes a continual call to study, think, reflect, and act. Through our Baptism and life of discipleship we will all become lifelong learners.

In most learning communities, our children are the main audience, often referred to as "the church of tomorrow." However, that perspective makes two mistakes about the learning community. First, it forgets that all children of God are the church of today and should rightfully be included as full participants in the learning community. Second, it implies that we impart a knowledge that the child will at some future date be able to renew and use. However, both children and adults best learn and appropriate those things that they can immediately use.

Nonetheless, within the learning community we do have a special responsibility to pass on the torch to the next generation. When we lose a parent through death, we realize that a part of our own remembered history also dies, because that parent knew a part of our life story that even we, the participants, do not know. Not only the events, but the interpretation and witness of those events from one generation to another must be shared as the living faith story.

You, your children, and your neighbors will come together in the learning community as mutual learners much in the way Letty Russell describes partnership:

> For Christians, partnership is to be understood as a relationship of mutuality and trust based on the gift of God's partnership with us in our lives. God has chosen to be partners with us as Immanuel so that we might become partners with ourselves, one another and with God.[4]

The learning community will enter into a relationship with one another that promotes a partnership of mutual learners and teachers who are faith sharers. Partnership learning encourages us to be mentors or midwives for one another in giving birth to those concepts, beliefs, and experiences that are a part of the faith journey. In all of this there will be opportunities for age- or interest-related experiences and learning. However, more attention should be given to the learning community that lives together and learns by reflection on its living. We learn forgiveness in the experience of asking for and receiving forgiveness. We understand anew the miracle of faith as the child accepts with awe, wonder, and joy the security found in our arms. We all learn some measure of God's love as we love and are received in love by our neighbor. The passage, "But let justice roll down like waters, and righteousness like an ever-flowing stream" (Amos 5:24), takes on life as we unite to work for justice in our community. We experience the hope of the resurrection in the funeral liturgy and through the care of one another.

For the church, our neighbors are not only those within the household, but also those along the way, and for these we must be an inclusive community. Jesus taught and had concern for a variety of people and was not constrained by the customs and rules of the day that despised some people or determined that some were so unclean that they did not even exist.

> The people who receive help from Jesus are therefore throughout, as the Gospels show, people on the fringe of society, men who because of fate, guilt or prevailing prejudice are looked upon as marked men, as outcasts: sick people who, according to the current doctrine of retribution, must bear their disease as a punishment for some sin committed; demoniacs, that is to say, those possessed of demons; those attacked by leprosy, "the first-born of death," to whom life in companionship with others is denied; Gentiles, who have no share in the privileges of Israel; women and children who do not count for anything in the community; and really bad people, the guilty, whom the good man assiduously holds at a distance.[5]

In daily life, the learning community meets the world of everyday people and everyday situations and experiences. The persons in the community encounter the people by the sea, in the houses, on the mountain. They reach out to the sick, the young, and the old. The learning community needs to be taught in a way that enables people to take the cross into their daily encounters as they share a friend's joy or sorrow, struggle with ethical dilemmas, use the world's resources, become active in current events of their community or world, speak for justice, or as they experience the gift of living and loving. It is in these daily encounters that the learning community spends most of its time. It is here that they find the greatest challenge to their faith and here that they struggle to see the God of Jesus Christ active in their lives.

Where the Learning Community Functions

". . . when you sit in your house, and when you walk by the way, and when you lie down, and when you rise."

The gathered community comes into its house for praise, nurture, refreshment, training, support, and service. All that the gathered community does should prepare its members to become the scattered who walk by the way. We come together to be sent out as the scattered people in the world. For the world is the place in which the people of God are sent for their daily mission. The learning community has three arenas—the home, parish-sponsored events with specific learning objectives, and other congregational functions—in which it has a specific responsibility to equip the gathered people for mission.

The home

The home unit is comprised in a variety of ways today. It is no longer the setting for just mother, father, and two children. The parish needs to be aware that one or more adults, with or without children, may comprise its home units. Society as a whole has assumed that the home is the basic educational and training unit, and the church has generally agreed with this conception. Yet in many of these home units people are uncomfortable or feel ill-prepared to be intentional about teaching, learning, and faith sharing. Few home units instruct in the traditional model of one person "teaching" another in a structured setting. Yet we know that teaching and learning best occur in the daily living situation when the words of instruction are given at the moment of need, which enables insight and application.

The church has always acknowledged the role of the home in the development of faith, yet this has been primarily a "should," with little sense of responsibility on the part of the parish and pastor. A learning community that includes the home unit will:

● include preparation for all persons to accept this privilege and responsibility;
● see that all classes and congregational programs provide resources for continuing learning in the home;
● provide study, devotional, and worship materials for home use;
● provide materials for home use that enable persons to be intentional about their remembering, studying, and reflecting on daily events (celebrations, conflicts, nature, community and world events, life

transitions, crises, and vacations) as God events and to see themselves as children of God living in mission.

Parish-sponsored events

Parish-sponsored classes, schools, programs, auxiliaries, retreats, and camps have an obvious learning function, which they carry out on behalf of the whole community. These learning functions will be articulated more fully in other chapters of this book. However, a few comments on these events from the total learning environment are in order within this chapter. The model from Deuteronomy 6 also suggests that these settings must be faithful to and consistent with the overall objective and mission of the church. The classroom also becomes a place in which the spirit and image ("spittin' image") of Jesus Christ is modeled and experienced as the students and teachers enter the learning setting with all their heart, soul, and might. Lifelong learners will become the norm, as opportunities for all ages are provided that seriously interface faith and daily life. These programs must be carefully planned so that the gathered people remember, correlate, interpret, and become the scattered people bursting to share the good news in every day and every place in which they "live and move and have [their] being" (Acts 17:28).

Other congregational functions

The learning community is involved in undergirding all other functions of the congregation. Perhaps this seems so obvious that, like the home, we've become careless and less intentional about this aspect of our lives. However, it is in this realm that we can be the most intentional learning community.

Worship comes alive, as the story, language, and symbols of our experience with God become the doorway through which we participate in the drama and encounter with God. Certainly, worship can be received as an art, a beautiful pageantry, and moving experience. But worship that is truly an engagement of people with their Lord and an appropriation for going "in peace" to "serve the Lord" will, by necessity, include an understanding of that worship. It will be important for the congregation to learn what takes place in worship, how the shape of worship is determined, the values that are conveyed through worship, and who is involved in worship. In addition, learning that undergirds worship will teach people to worship in small group and individual settings and provide the tools for personal devotional life.

God's people participate in ministries of loving *service* as a response not only to God's will, but more importantly to the love shown by God through Jesus Christ. This community will encourage corporate acts of service, individual service, and a linking with other agencies within the community and around the world. Servanthood for all members of the community will be encouraged at their level of understanding and ability. It will call people to an understanding of justice and service that seeks to eliminate oppression, exploitation, and injustice. This will be a learning-for-servanthood model that enables all people to make their decisions, take up the cross, and follow in the way of the gospel. Because God has given us glimpses of the kingdom and because of our longing for peace and justice, we seek shalom through our service.

The *witness* function of many congregations is performed by a group of people who meet monthly to receive motivation and tips on how to make calls, report on their visitation activities of the past month, and receive assignments for future visits. Often, visitors see their primary task as making a friendly call and telling about their parish. While these meeting and visitation styles are not wrong, they are woefully incomplete. Perhaps we have difficulty recruiting people for this task because they think they will have to be salespeople, and they feel inadequate for the task. To amend this problem, the primary learning role of witness committees should be to come together to study, share, and reflect on one's faith with the express purpose of becoming more equipped to go out and intentionally share that faith to specific people on behalf of the congregation.

In addition, the church's witness cannot be limited to appointed committees, however well they function. All people—from the youngest to the oldest—can learn what it means to personally share the faith. Jesus was never content with just walking among the people or hoping that folks would know his mission or message by his daily life and routine—nor should we ever be. All that he did—from daily events such as meals or walking with his friends to healing and miracles—always furthered the proclamation of the kingdom.

We may say about a special event, "When I hear, you'll know, because I'll shout it from the rooftops." Our learning community can equip and motivate its people to shout the good news from the rooftops as people whose physical presence mirrors the good news and whose words and actions intentionally speak and give life to the good news.

Supporting the mission of God's people, while essential, can easily become mechanistic. But, as learning undergirds these functions:

- discipleship, rather than volunteerism, will characterize the stewardship life of the congregation. Jesus did not call the disciples to be volunteers, nor were they commissioned to "Go and make volunteers." Our Baptism begins a life of commitment to the body that sets it apart from all other commitments we make. The tasks of the community—teaching, cleaning, visiting, leading worship, etc.—as well as the tasks of the individual in daily life, come out of that understanding.

- stewardship committees will continue to be faithful to wise financial practices, but will place first priority on understanding the call for this congregation and how dollars support that call. They will keep congregational learning at the heart of stewardship development.

- learning for stewardship will give equal importance to time, talents, and dollars.

- the congregation will adopt a stewardship call that supports its gathered life only as that is equipping them to be the scattered people with a mission.

- buildings, equipment, publicity, and literature will be statements of the community's values and mission.

Methods of the Learning Community

". . . teach them diligently . . . talk to them . . . bind them as a sign . . . write them. . . ."

In describing the teaching/learning style the writer of Deuteronomy used language that suggests the all-encompassing nature of the command. The commandment was to be intentionally taught, it was to be written and spoken, and it was to be visible to all those whom Israel met. The commandment implied more than a Sabbath observance; its observance became an integral part of the life of the community.

This type of observance calls for an intentionality that is related to our objective, nature, participants, context, and methods. It reminds us that we are never to lose sight of our objective as we incorporate it into every aspect of our activities, relationships, and our very being. An intentional learning community will be aware that the formal and informal settings, play and study, content and experience, daily life and parish life require attention and become opportunities for the Christian's encounter with the gospel.

Sometimes we hear Christians say, "I don't ever *say* I'm a Christian; others will know by my life-style." Or, perhaps we have heard our friends express hesitation about sharing the good news for fear they may offend. In like manner, we often hear church leaders, particularly with youth events, attempting to entice participants by fancy events and fun activities. The learning community can certainly play together, but this should never be a cover-up for the hope that "once we get them here," or "once we become friends," then our "real" purpose can be expressed. The learning community will always be faithful to its purpose and be intentional in all settings.

The learning community will also equip its members not merely to know some answers, but to begin to think theologically. Paul Tillich reminds us that who we are compels us to think theologically.

> Being human means asking the questions of one's own being and living under the impact of the answers given to this question. And, conversely, being human means receiving answers to the question of one's own being and asking questions under the impact of the answers.[6]

> Therefore, every religious educator must try to find the existentially important questions which are alive in the minds and hearts of the pupils. It must make the pupil aware of the questions which he already has.[7]

The rate at which changes are made in today's society, the complexities of ethical issues, and the mobility we experience make simplistic or pat answers obsolete almost before they are spoken. The environment that encourages questions, dialogs about answers, and explores options—always within its calling to be the children of God in mission—will free people to use their theological resources at all times.

Another characteristic of this learning community will be that its method is based on incarnational engagement. The Deuteronomic writer did not call Israel to an objective knowledge of God, but rather to a dialog, a relationship that gives meaning to all of life. Christ is an *event* of birth, death, and life to which the disciple is invited to share. The community will understand and express God's continuing activity and revelation as an experience in which they belong.

This learning community is bound by its calling to be the people of God, the new creation. As the new creation, they unite with all their heart, mind, and soul to be in the spirit and image of God gathered as a family of faith for intentional remembering, reflection, interpretation, and becoming the scattered people in the world.

FOUR

THE COMMUNITY OF FAITH AS CURRICULUM

Norma J. Everist

The learning community is the spirit and image of the creating, redeeming, sanctifying God. This community of faith *is* the curriculum: God and God's people in this time and place. The entire worship, service, and witness life of the community is context and content of Christian education. In this chapter we shall look at this community of faith, beginning with Christ as the center and seeing that it is by grace we have become a community that can teach and learn from one another. We shall then consider how we set up the learning environment, including the law-and-gospel dimension of that environment and of the teaching/learning activities. Exploring the formative effects of the worlds in which we live, "this time and place," we shall try to make connections so that we can educate for mission. Finally, we shall speak about selecting methods and about mutual accountability.

The Center: Christ

Some learning, such as algebra, must by its nature be linear and sequential. This is not the nature of the Christian faith. We do not teach so that students know the right facts, so that they perform good works, so they can earn an *A* from God. All that is necessary for salvation and faith is already complete in the incarnation, death, and resurrection of Jesus Christ.

Is there, then, nothing left for Christian education to do? There is everything to do, and Christ is the beginning. Whatever learning takes place spirals out from that center.[1] It begins in our Baptism in Christ, and in it we already have received the complete gift. Now we unwrap it to treasure it and use it in Christian living.

Our teaching will be carefully planned. However, we also will be ready to utilize any present life experience in our learning, trusting that God's Spirit is alive and active among us.[2] In our teaching we shall strive to build skills for witness, but we shall recognize that by grace each learner is already a minister. Our teaching will have goals and objectives, but evaluation will not depend on having finished the page or "done" the book. Learners will grow and gain much, but such learning will result in their giving themselves in servanthood. The course is already complete in Christ, which means we are now free to begin.

The Community of Faith

We view the community of faith in terms of creation, redemption, and sanctification. Believing that a good God created this world for interdependence rather than for competitive aggression, we teach in the Creator's mode when we teach not to pit one student against another, but so that each learner will be more whole and more able. Likewise, the teacher need not fear nor control the student's emerging ability. The teacher can even become the learner, and the learner the teacher. There are global implications for this model of interdependence. An individual, a class, a church, or a nation is created to develop fully, not to overpower another, but so that all peoples, strong and able, can live interdependently in God's world.

God's people also disappoint and hurt one another. They are bickering and broken. At times one called to minister in the community of faith doubts that this is the body of Christ; they are more like Hosea's "not my people."[3] How can one teach when adults aren't speaking to one another, or when children won't sit still, or when neither comes to class?

It is precisely at that time, the right time, Paul's letter to the Romans reminds us, that Christ becomes the power for reconciliation.[4] By God's grace our own dreams of community are shattered and God mercifully names this people of God by Christ's name.[5] Believing that "not my people" has become God's people, receiving mercy to become teachers and learners in interdependent ways is the beginning of educational ministry.

The awkward Bible campers are people in whom the Spirit of God dwells. The recalcitrant trustees who will not see the theological ramifications of their work are elbows and arms in the body of Christ. The depressed young adult, feeling betrayed by the world and wondering, *Because I am not the person they thought I should become, do I fit in this church?* is not less part of the body. The screaming, baptized baby is a worker with us.[6] The very hardest part of teaching may be believing. Once we, by the power of the Spirit, believe that this motley group in this out-of-the way congregation is the body of Christ, called to learn that they might minister, there are no limits to growth potential. Believing I am God's created one—often unfaithful, yet always loved and restored to community—enables me to teach faithfully.

Teaching to Learn and Learning to Teach

A question frequently asked of church councils is, "How many teachers do we have this year?" Answers bring sighs of relief, or commiseration followed by desperate attempts to recruit. The appropriate answer is that everyone in the community of faith is a teacher. People may not know they are teaching by the things they say and do, and their action or inaction may be "false" doctrine, or the core of the gospel, but they are teaching, nonetheless. People teach in the very act of being born. We learn through watching someone die. A man said, "My mother's last words, to her son whom she no longer recognized at her bedside were, 'Thank you, Jesus!' " Our postures of praise teach the newcomer, and our ways of making committee decisions teach what we believe about each other and the church. Our calls inform; they also teach skills of demeaning gossip or compassionate care. Intergenerationally, we watch and learn the struggle of faith in God's steadfast love.

Recruitment for formal classroom teaching might begin with an affirmation of the ongoing and pervasive nature of our teaching and learning throughout all of our activity in the congregation and in the world. The question then is not, "Whose arm can we twist to teach this year?" but, "*How* do you intend to teach this year?" We might ask each member of the congregation, "How do you like to teach?" and, "How do you like to learn?" In such an approach we see that the classroom is only one setting among an infinite possibility of learning environments.

In our daily life in the world we are continually learning. Rather than shun the world, we might learn reflective tools for making sense of such learning and discerning it theologically, a process to be discussed later in this chapter. Christians are also teaching in these worlds, though we may not believe we have much influence there. Rather than remain in a constant state of guilt over our ineffectual attempts at evangelism, we might use our time together as the gathered people of God to share, nurture, suggest, and strengthen one another as we go forth to be teachers as the scattered people of God in our daily worlds.

We may compliment the teenager who refrains from going along with peers' use of drugs, but do we also converse with the youth who speak out in their social-studies classes on issues of war and hunger and economics, basing their views on the faith they are learning to articulate through their confirmation classes? The young child in fourth-grade art class in public school is invited to draw a picture expressing a view of his or her neighborhood, and the Christian child quite naturally draws the local congregation into the picture. Rather than insisting that children be taught to pray in public school, how do we encourage such children simply to express the fact that God makes a difference in their lives as they seek to be a community of diverse people in the public world called "neighborhood"? The adult in the office or at the farm implement store or at the Red Cross meeting is learning and teaching. We need each other's help as we discern our teaching ministries of interpretation, advocacy, change, and care.[7] This, too, is curriculum.

Some congregations are incorporating the mentor relationship in their confirmation-ministry program,[8] thereby linking the informal ways we teach and learn from one another with the formal classroom teaching. We thereby recognize the broader possibilities of teaching and learning, while enriching our traditional classroom settings. In this more systematic way we develop plans for fulfilling our educational ministry. Our classes may be age grouped, but they involve persons throughout their life span. We have an instructional component, but there are nurturing and vocational components as well.[9]

Learning to teach is crucial for formal classroom settings. Donald Griggs, who has produced so many helpful materials for church school teachers, summarizes those teaching tasks as building relationships, encouraging participation and interaction, planning for teaching with curriculum, developing biblical skills, enabling creativity, using audiovisuals, and nurturing faith.[10] Relational skills involve more than being friendly; teachers encourage cooperation, teamwork, and sharing. Teachers encourage participation through good use of questions and through realizing the importance of students making choices. Teachers learn to plan by considering the time, space, and resources; by setting objectives; and by selecting teaching activities and developing strategies.[11]

Teachers often report they have learned more in the midst of teaching than they ever imagined. The tenets of the faith become theirs in powerful new ways. Likewise, having been together in creative ways in the classroom, learners inevitably go forth to teach. There are infinite grouping possibilities and arenas in the world for our cyclical educational ministry. The question to ask is simply, How can we who belong to this faith community learn to teach, and teach in order to learn?

Setting the Learning Environment

We have considered the "God and God's people" half of our definition of curriculum. We need to give attention to "in this time and place." The learning environment is the entire culture in which we live. Before exploring the broader context, we need to look at the classroom, where, for many teachers "getting attention" is the frustrating, central problem. Learners observe this and continue to insist on new ways the teacher will entertain. Meanwhile, teachers wear out countless methods and resources, complaining that none of them works.

The one failure may be in establishing the learning environment. A wide variety of materials will be useful, and most methods will work if the class has become a trusting community of learners. We need a learning environment with trustworthy boundaries of space and time. It needs to be physically, emotionally, and intellectually trustworthy.

Do we wonder why the class has a hard time settling down when the teacher breathlessly runs into class late? Do we find ourselves yelling, or, with older students, using snide or guilt-producing remarks to control? The leader has the responsibility for setting the learning environment. Abdication of teaching authority at this point disables the learners. Once the learning environment is established, however, the community itself helps maintain a disciplined atmosphere.

We need to give attention to physical matters such as size of room, shape of chair arrangement, lighting, color, temperature. Will we need tables, or should we all sit on the floor? If the chairs are too small or the room too warm, adults simply will not return. We create colorful rooms for kindergarten children, but expect that bare walls will do for adults. We may not necessarily need bigger, better facilities. The congregation as learning community can look at what they have and creatively decide how a small room can be just right for a particular intimate grouping, or how one might create a loft in a high-ceilinged fellowship hall. The physical surroundings, mutually chosen, can signal that we are ready for stimulating interaction with one another.

Time is a gift. We need to respect each other's time, selecting a time of day, week, or year that is appropriate for the needs of this particular people. Would a late-afternoon vacation school be better than mornings in this community? Would a noontime book study open our church's educational ministry to business people in the area?

We structure learning environments for outreach, while not neglecting the individual. Why do we dismiss class because only one child came? That one person's timely presence needs to be respected. A teacher's faithful presence is crucial. A cadre of substitutes can be trained so that in case of illness neither class nor teacher are left confused. We wonder why people refuse to teach a second year when doubling up classes at the last moment has become the common practice. With mutual respect for each other's time and healthy time-learning boundaries, learning is enhanced and faithfulness encouraged.

The learning environment needs to be intellectually trustworthy. By giving attention to developmental stages of learners, we can listen for their level of language, vocabulary, and reasoning. If the environment is beyond the intellectual capabilities, the group will grow embarrassed and discouraged. But if it is too simple (a mistaken idea of "safe"), the learners will not be able to work at their growing edge so that they are prepared to live and speak in the public world. With a trustworthy learning environment, no question will be "stupid" and no idea threatening. If the boundaries are safe, the learners will be able to take risks necessary for growth.

Emotionally and psychologically the learning environment must be trustworthy. That commitment requires confidentiality. The child's feelings and privacy need to be respected, just like an adult's. Learners can grow to trust that they can bring to class what's really on their hearts as well as their minds. We invite, but do not cajole, manipulate, or "volunteer" people to speak; we respect and receive them. The learning community grows to respect one another, and each learns that this is a place where important things are expected to happen.

The Law-and-Gospel Dimension

There is a law-and-gospel dimension to setting the learning environment. When we hear law and gospel proclaimed in a sermon, we may grow accustomed to a predictable pattern. At 11:12 A.M. we will hear that we are sinners, and at 11:23 we will hear that Jesus died for our sins. Good preaching, of course, will not be that predictable. The point is that the dialogical nature of teaching and learning permits participants to engage in a law-and-gospel dynamic that cannot happen when only the pastor is speaking. We often miss that potential and settle to merely teach *about* the faith or learn moralisms.

In setting the learning environment, some teachers believe that the main goal is to capture and hold attention. The result is that students learn that their good behavior is what pleases the teacher, and no doubt God as well. No matter what the lesson for the day, such a teaching environment is already legalistic. We misuse the law. We may also misinterpret the gospel, believing that grace and mercy mean "anything goes." We tolerate any rebellious, hurtful behavior, barely holding our own resentment in check, and call that "love." We also misrepresent the gospel when we believe Christian learners are "nice," thereby discouraging people from coming in grubby work clothes and bringing their real selves, complete with their grubby natures of fear, hatred, anger, and pain.

The law-and-gospel dimension has a more faithful meaning for our learning community. The law can be used as a curb, a guard that prevents us from hurting and being hurt. We employ this simply to provide a safe and trustworthy learning environment. An extreme example is the congregation that asked, "What shall we do? We're having trouble with our classes!" When invited to describe the problem, they said, "The children leave class to go to the store to buy candy during the session, and they could get hurt crossing that busy street." One must set some boundaries so that the children don't leave class. We therefore caringly set the temporal, physical, emotional, and intellectual learning boundaries of which we have spoken.

Correspondingly, there is a gospel dimension to the learning environment. It relates to the First Article of the Apostles' and Nicene Creeds, and to the Second and Third Articles as well. God's loving, orderly creation and God's unconditional love of the individual and of the community are what define the environment. Such gospel encircling means we bring to the time and place together all that we are; nothing need be left behind nor hidden. No teaching method creates faith, but each can be used as the Spirit moves. By grace God forms a community of faith, a learning environment, so that by the Spirit's power, faith can come forth. Centered in Christ and surrounded by God's love, we can dare to be known, for instead of moralism or legalism, forgiveness is present, and our bondages of separation are replaced by reconciliation.

Another use of the law convicts, showing me my sin and pointing me once more, surprisingly, marvelously, to the gospel. When the learning environment has been set, this dynamic can happen. We know brokenness will be present in the people who come, so the word of forgiveness and new life will need to be spoken, but the particular words and the particular experience will not be predictable.

One need not beat people over the head with the law. If we have invited people really to be present, the brokenness of the world will come too, whether it be in disillusionment, or fear, or regret, or remorse of the smallest child or the eldest parishioner. We should not so much teach that we break the law, as that we break ourselves and each other on God's law. With the law's presence, remorse is turned to contrition, and the learner once again is able to see a need for the gospel.

Likewise, in this trustworthy setting, the power of the gospel can be released. Rather than talking about the gospel, as though it happened only to holy people long ago, or memorizing a Bible passage only because we might need it someday in the future, we can speak and act on the power of the gospel now, as it relates to the pain and the problem of the moment. To do this we will need to listen to each other, and we will need continually to listen to the Word so that its truth might be relevant in this relationship. Christ never said, "Take up your bed and walk" to a person who was blind, nor, "You can see" to someone who was lame.[12] The gospel is real and powerful for hurting people. Our educational ministry will need to be real as well.

We shall not so much learn the text as learn that the text knows us. The Christ, who is at the center at each stage of our lives, encounters us this day in the text once again. For example, in the feeding stories in the Gospels, there is food for all. To an adult burdened with the responsibility for feeding one's family, having just lost a job or the farm, the good news is that Christ knows our hunger and our poverty, and even our worry and embarrassment. For the child the good news in this session is significance, for it is the child's gifts that are used to feed the masses. The good news for all is that Christ has compassion and gives them bread to feed each other. That's gospel action. That's educational ministry.

The Broader Learning Context

We who carry the Word and are carried by it interact with the Word in the present moment.[13] The God of history is the God of today. All of our teaching is therefore existential. We neither simply study about

God's past heroes and heroines nor employ a banking system, depositing information to be drawn on in later life.[14] God, however, is not limited to our situation and our experience. God is transcendent and will not be created in our image.

God is God and brings to this moment and space all the creative forces of the universe and all of history. God is surely present in this place among us but this God is also present and active in every other place. The tradition, particularly the biblical tradition, informs us as to the nature of God and God's interaction in the past. The Christ event focuses that history.

The curriculum, which is God at work among us in this place, has global dimensions as well. But God is not simply out there among others. By taking seriously the power of God that creates, forgives, and changes us in this time and place, we are able to see God's length and breadth, all the world and all history, including God's promised future. This means we need not limit our learning. We need not be alienated from the past nor fear the future. We can look beyond the classroom walls.

As teachers and learners in God's interdependent world, we are held in God's hands. We are never outside God's knowing and care. This is the ultimate, trustworthy learning environment, even when all my senses tell me, "This situation cannot be trusted." God is graciously creating neighborhoods so that we can learn to be different together. We need each other, even each other's handicaps, for none of us is whole. All the world is God's classroom, a gigantic heterogeneous grouping of men and women, boys and girls, North and South, East and West, ebony and ivory and bronze hues, disabilities and abilities. The curriculum is God and God's people all over the place. God loves this company of strangers, enabling us not only to live together but to learn from one another.[15]

Attending the Context and Making Connections

Learning together is a matter of making connections. The creating, redeeming, and life-giving God continues graciously to reach out to us. God is teaching, but we have other teachers as well. The world in which we live shapes us. All that we do teaches profoundly. Teaching and learning is making a connection between the catechetical "What does this mean?" of God's Word and the "What in the world does this mean?" of our own lives.

A young child hears "God loves you," but experiences physical abuse. A grade-school child readily agrees to the commandments the class just learned, but feels a strange inner joy at having snitched on a classmate. A young adult, equipped for a career, faces competing value systems of family, friends, and employer. At this point in life what does Christ's "follow me" mean? A person in midlife has suddenly lost a sense of meaning in her life's work, and an older adult, missing peers, discovers he is often more despairing than he would like to be. God's *shalom* is elusive.

Through the life cycle, "What in the world does this mean?" is an ever-changing, but always present, question. Luther's simple yet profound catechetical question, "What does this mean?" intersects with who we are and what we bring to this learning community at this present moment. That intersection is the place for dynamic learning.[16]

How does the community of faith make these connections? It does so by giving attention to, or "attending" the biblical tradition, the cultural influence, and our own experience.[17] The biblical witness may seem distant, so we, as a community of faith, must attend it carefully, without taming it to make it more compatible with our life-style. God's will is hidden, in the sense that God's unconditional love is never our expectation, but it is always being revealed through Word and sacrament in the Christian community. The biblical tradition is consistent, yet multifaceted. Layers of biblical interpretation and the diverse ways God's people have responded to that Word mean we must listen to the context of tradition rather than settle for "the way we've always taught it."[18]

We attend the Word, because we so very much need to hear that word of forgiveness and hope in a world seemingly gone mad. The world does not want us to know that. There are words of hope from our civil faith, but they are false hope. Nonetheless, we listen, and often believe. Advertisements appeal to our cultural belief system in such phrases as, "Comfort is the key," "Buy yourself a little happiness—you deserve it," or, "Be in control with. . . ."

Even though we may not purchase that product, the culture is shaping our belief systems. Because I have grown up in a particular place in a particular time, I construct reality in a certain way. Theological reflection in a Christian learning community enables me to attend the context, to listen to that which has shaped and is shaping me, so that I might examine its power.

The process is cyclical, not linear. Part of the curriculum is the person, raised by a certain family, in a certain culture, shaped by world events, yet a unique individual with personal experiences. The person I am teaches the person I am becoming. I am trained for work, but my work also teaches me.[19] As we help learners attend their own experiences, we are readied to meet the Word, making connections so that the pain and the promise, the law and the gospel, teach in the present.

The present is never isolated; even the context has its own context. The Word and the world come to us shaped by God's historic and global activity. So, too, the connections made in this curricular moment send us forth to live once more in our worlds. The curriculum is God and God's people in this time and place, and yet even this dynamic moment of making connections has a broader context. A nursing home provides one example. The older adults in this setting have their own present identity. However, all the previous stages of their lives are present as well. How the learners encountered the Word in years past is brought to this "classroom" today. The use of fantasy for reflection helps bring to this present moment their many previous contexts. I have seen ripples of learning after the "teacher" has left the building as these elderly learners talk and remember and think and relate and make new connections of faith in their lives.

Education Is for Mission

How does one measure such contextual education? It must be measured in terms of mission. Christian education is for mission.[20] Because we have been joined with Jesus the Christ in Baptism, we are free to serve, to risk, to speak, and to act in care for others. Education, therefore, is always an equipping task, not a conserving activity. We learn so that we might live. God's Word becomes real in and among us so that we, by God's grace, might carry it in the world.

Learners are already active in the world. Rather than telling students to apply the truth in their lives or goading people with guilt to evangelize, we do well to reflect on the missions in which the learners are already engaged. Even the young child, through Baptism, is already a ministering child.[21] The question is, What are people believing based on the mission in which they are engaged? If my mission this week is to secure my future, I will purchase more insurance and vote to tighten zoning laws to prevent a halfway house from being established in my neighborhood. If my goal this week is to win recognition so that I can feel better about myself, I may try to monopolize the teacher's attention or dress uniquely (or outrageously, depending on the viewpoint), or act in an exemplary or recalcitrant way, for if I cannot obtain positive recognition, negative is better than none.

These "missions" testify to our belief system and, therefore, to our gods. Such gods will betray me, because my own efforts to secure myself never will be foolproof. Even if I succeed in gaining attention, such a spotlight also will illumine my fallibility. Even gaining the attention of one special person whom I admire may turn to dust, for that person cannot be my god.

When, however, the gospel is being shared in the community of faith, God once again replaces false gods, and my mission will change—not totally, but perceptively. Believing my future and my present are secure in the steadfast love of a covenant God who will not forsake me, I can purchase or not purchase insurance. The matter is loosed of its ultimate power in my life. I can listen to many sides on a zoning issue and decide with compassion. If my worth is grounded in God who has called and named me, if I always have the attention of the one before whom all angels bow, I will be able to dress and behave for the sake of others. My dress will not deprecate myself in unbelief nor overwhelm the other whom I am now free to serve.

Christian education that listens to the context and helps participants make connections between the Word and the world will deal with the basic question of, Who is my god? Cutting through the chaos and empowering us with the gospel, such education will result in new missions.

Teaching Methodologies

If through careful setting of the learning environment, one is freed from selecting methods in order to *keep* attention, so that one might *give* attention to the biblical tradition, the cultural influences, and the learners' experiences, methods can be chosen on the basis of style appropriate to the learning objectives. Many educational approaches think about objectives in terms of (1) cognitive, (2) affective, and (3) action. We expect something to happen intellectually, emotionally, and in areas of mission skill building.

Each of these areas has multiple levels. The methodology should match the learning objective. For example, using a crossword puzzle of names of African cities (because it is fun and easy to do) to meet an affective learning objective "to become sensitive to oppression in Third World countries" would be inappropriate, but a "word find" on Old Testament biblical books would meet the cognitive objective "to become acquainted with name of minor prophets."

In lesson planning, the infinitive form of verbs clarifies and opens possibilities. The reader is invited to add to this sample list:

Cognitive	Affective	Action
To recognize . . .	To hold in awe . . .	To be able to pray *ex corde* . . .
To understand . . .	To enjoy . . .	To listen for . . .
To compare . . .	To appreciate . . .	To speak a caring word to . . .
To question . . .	To empathize with . . .	To be able to act on . . .
To integrate . . .	To feel our fear of . . .	To organize people to . . .

Each of these could be completed so that the objective is specific and attainable. One learning objective for fourth grade might be, "To be able to pray *ex corde* one sentence in a group circle prayer." At a ninth grade level, in relation to a study of the Psalms, one might have cognitive, affective, and action objectives: "To be aware this week of my own feelings of joy, anger, and frustration," "To integrate contemporary words of praise and lament with the ancient Psalter," and, "To be able to write a contemporary psalm to be used in worship next month."

Once free to select methodology in relation to learning objectives, the community of faith can use large-group or one-on-one discussion in the classroom, build role-model or mentor learning relationships outside the classroom, go on field trips to the learners' worlds, or use video tapes or biblical simulation. In each methodology there are theological implications. In selecting discussion we say theologically that each person is someone in whom the Spirit dwells. The task is one of a midwife, helping the person give birth to that which is already inside. But the totality of truth is inside no one human being. We use lecture and storytelling to bring to the present moment the Word of God outside ourselves and our experience. Experiential learning, a powerful teaching/learning mode, testifies to the incarnational Christ, who came in the flesh and walked with people. Our learning can also utilize and simulate our human experiences. Confrontational methods, not to be chosen for discipline or control purposes, can witness to the fact that the Christian's life confronts competing values and gods and therefore requires clarification.

Our view of the faith community informs our methodological assumptions. A teacher who assumes that the student is a sinner, totally unable to act in a holy way, will set about the task of conversion. A teacher who believes the child is in need of information in order to learn how to act in Christian ways will try to impart ideas and modify behavior. The teacher who assumes the learners need to discover their own potential will rely totally on open-ended discussion.[22] Each methodology reflects only part of the truth. A rich diversity of learning objectives and methods will express the theologically complex nature of the community of faith. The educational minister is called to be theologian, educator, and administrator, as well as teacher of teachers, in this all-encompassing calling of ongoing nurturing and equipping.

Mutual Accountability

Mutual accountability develops out of concern for one another. Rather than saying, "He missed last time, I can miss this time," a group learned of an emergency in the life of one member, called each other, and made arrangements to meet another time as well as to respond to the present emergency. A small or struggling congregation may have a blessed position, because their need for another is so obvious, but in larger congregations small groups can accomplish the same purpose.

Many studies have shown that students will live up or down to teacher expectations. The Christian learning community that expects each member to come ready for dynamic law/gospel interchange will find that people come ready to do so, bringing Scripture and life experience with them. The smallest child knows if the teacher really wants to hear what has happened all week. The adult-class members who take each other's vocations seriously will not begin with gossip, but may bring newspaper editorials and may ask each other to help in decision making.

We will encourage one another to grow at our learning edge, but respect the fact that we will be at different places, perhaps in different political parties or on different sides on a school or community issue. We can welcome that diversity, knowing that we stand together with Christ in the center. I do not expect you to become like me. Our mutual accountability is linked in Christ. With that expectation we will be growing outward from that center, perhaps in some ways moving away from each other, as we go forth into our diverse worlds. We return, however, to the center, which is Christ and Christ's worshiping, teaching/learning community.

Our growth will be measured in ministry and mission. Perhaps we now know how to serve church dinners and send cards to parents of new babies. How do we build on those ministry skills to learn how to care for the physical, psychological, and spiritual needs of grieving people? We have leadership skills for congregational committees and we read newspapers about injustice. How do we put those skills and that concern together to organize so that our concern for Namibia will follow through in mission action?

The community of faith will continue to have broken relationships within the community that need healing. As the reconciled faith community of Christ, with expectations that the Spirit is at work, there also will be signs of mutual growth and of making dynamic connection for life and mission in the world. By grace we already are this people of God, this curriculum.

FIVE

INTERACTION OF FAITH AND CULTURE

Erwin Buck

Culture as the Matrix of Communication

Communication between people of different cultures involves a never-ending process of translating not only words but entire value systems. One culture differs from another in language, ideas, beliefs, presuppositions, habits, customs, social organization, values, and in many other ways. These differences are not superficial and should not be minimized. They affect a society's basic approach to reality as a whole. An immigrant to a new land inevitably experiences "culture shock."

Just as important as the spoken words are the presuppositions, which are not expressed because they are taken for granted in a given cultural milieu. To a Hebrew, the word *Torah* conjures up a multitude of associations that can hardly be communicated to a Gentile. The unwritten message between the lines is at least as important as are the written words. Language is inextricably embedded in a cultural matrix. Communication is therefore always a complex cultural phenomenon. The way we think, act, and speak is largely conditioned by the culture that we have inherited. In this respect Christians are not very different from non-Christians. One of the earliest Christian documents, the Letter to Diognetus, acknowledges frankly that Christians follow "the customs of the natives in respect of clothing, food and the rest of their ordinary conduct."

The good news inevitably bears the imprint of the country in which it is proclaimed.

The implications of what has been said so far are mind-boggling. If all communication is culturally conditioned, then there can be no divine revelation that is not tied to culture in an inextricable way. The doctrine of the incarnation affirms that God steps into history, takes on flesh, and communicates with us in our human language. God operates within the coordinates of human existence and submits to the limitations of time and space, language, and culture. Jesus was born a Jew and raised according to Jewish custom, so that even the revelation that comes through Jesus bears the marks of a particular culture. Paul, too, needed to be a Jew to the Jews, but a Gentile to the Gentiles (1 Cor. 9:20).

If God sends signals that are not culturally conditioned, none of us is able to receive them, since our eyes and ears, our sensory organs, and our minds can respond to only a limited range of stimuli. God must communicate within that range or else fail to communicate with us. This is both the glory and the cross of an incarnational theology.

In a feudal system one can make meaningful theological statements by describing Christ variously as master or servant. In a society familiar with the institution of slavery it makes sense to speak of believers as slaves or as free persons or as both. A society that thinks of illness as the result of demonic activity will experience healing as the exorcism of demons. One can speak to such societies by using other categories, of course, but the people will perceive other worldviews as strange or unacceptable. The experience of Galileo vividly illustrates what happens when one worldview encounters another.

Some concepts that are at home in one particular culture cannot be expressed at all in another. The Greeks delighted in long discussions regarding the "substance" or "essence" of a desk, a tree, or an acorn. In a Hebraic context such talk is meaningless. Correspondingly, Judaism, which regards all "natural phenomena" as the result of God's personal and powerful activity in the world, has no room for such concepts as "laws of nature" or "miracle," if "miracle" is understood in the popular sense as the breaking of some "law of nature."

To complicate matters still further, cultures are not static, so that the phenomenon of "culture shock" can also be experienced by people who never leave their native land. Any given culture undergoes changes, sometimes imperceptibly, sometimes rather violently. Even language undergoes significant changes. We may recall a time, not so long ago, when the word *man* was understood as an inclusive term and when references to God in the male gender represented the unquestioned norm.

Within any one given culture, people often migrate from one subculture to another and change their views and presuppositions as they go. Members of the "youth culture," who rallied to the shout, "Don't trust anyone over 30," suddenly and dramatically altered their tune when they reached their 30th birthdays.

To summarize: communication is inextricably embedded in a cultural setting. Every document—Bible, creeds, and confessions included—expresses the Christian faith in terms congenial to the culture of a particular day and place.

Characteristics of First-Century Culture

The process of cultural development and migration has gone on for 2000 years since the appearance of the Christ and the compilation of the Christian scriptural canon. Not necessarily have we become wiser or better in the process, but we have moved a great distance in time and space.

When we open our Bibles or study our Christian tradition, we might think of ourselves as immigrants in a strange land. The modern reader cannot hope to understand the Bible without some awareness of the complex world in which these books were produced.

To begin to understand that world, we must at least make an honest attempt to divest ourselves of the cultural agglomeration of the past two millenia. A few examples may illustrate how different a world it was.

Matthew sensed no difficulty in relating a story involving a star that moved and stopped so as to give travel directions. Luke took it for granted that a fetus in a womb could respond joyfully to the presence of his yet unborn Lord. Luke was not embarrassed by a report that the sun darkened at noon at Passover time (even though a solar eclipse cannot occur when the moon is full), and Matthew could visualize dead people walking the streets of Jerusalem after the death of Jesus.

In these respects Matthew and Luke are not very different from other writers of the time. Practically all of the above phenomena can be duplicated from non-Christian literature of the period. To the modern reader at home in Western society, however, such stories present a significant problem, and when Hebrews 9:22 asserts that "without the shedding of blood there is no forgiveness," many modern Christians find it difficult to give their assent to the proposition.

In the first century the idea of truth was defined differently from the way we conceive of it in an age preoccupied with science. First-century society was also clearly not concerned with history in the sense in which we now define it.

The purpose of reports then was not in the first place to establish what actually happened. The aim of story was to edify and encourage faith and devotion. Correspondingly, the practice of pseudepigraphy was widely accepted and did not carry the modern connotation of "forgery" and something similar applies in the case of what today might be termed "plagiarism." Copyright laws are, after all, a very recent development. The fear of evil spirits was rampant in Greek as well as in Jewish circles, and illness could be cured by visiting a sanctuary or by exorcism.

In addition, it must be noted that the Christian society of the first century was not altogether uniform. Within the New Testament itself we find a great variety of viewpoints, each representing, no doubt, various subgroups within the larger unit. For example, one can detect traces of an ascetic emphasis, which under certain conditions even counseled the amputation of an offending hand or foot (Mark 9:42), although this was most likely not intended to be taken literally. On the other hand, there are clear indications that Jesus and his disciples did not practice an ascetic way of life.

In a similar vein, being a true follower of Jesus may in one milieu require that one "hate" even one's wife and children (Luke 14:26ff.), but at another time and place it imposes a deeper responsibility for the care of dependents (Col. 3:18—4:1). With respect to political authority we find equally diverse traditions recorded. Romans 13 counsels submission to the powers that be, since they are all instituted by God, a view that is well-represented in Hellenism by Socrates, who readily committed suicide when the authorities ordered him to do so. Revelation 13, on the other hand, regards the secular authority as demonic, a view that is well-attested in Jewish apocalyptic literature. The same variety that characterized Jewish and pagan society of the first century can thus also be found in the pages of the New Testament.

Some writers, such as Paul, expected the end of the world and the breaking in of the kingdom of God almost momentarily, whereas other documents, such as the book of Revelation, anticipated a much more drawn-out process, even involving a 1000-year interim period. Some authors told the story of Jesus in terms of a vicarious sacrifice for sin, whereas others portrayed it as a victory over demonic powers.

In summary, there is a considerable distance between the cultural presuppositions of the first century and those of modern, western civilization. Furthermore, even within the pages of the New Testament one finds not just one set of cultural coordinates, but several. To say this is not to pass a value judgment on the one or on the other, but only to make an observation and to issue a note of caution: what is said in the context of one cultural milieu is not always directly applicable to another.

Biblical Faith in Transition between Cultures

Since human culture is always in a state of flux, it is only to be expected that the divine revelation that was addressed to one particular historical and cultural milieu cannot simply be transferred to another without appropriate modification and adjustment. Judaism, too, sensed that the laws of the Old Testament, together with its customs, needed to be adapted to fit the situation of a later period. Much of the *Mishna* is designed precisely to meet that need.

Let one example suffice as an illustration. According to the *Torah*, a stubborn and rebellious son was to be stoned (Deut. 21:18-21). Later Judaism, of course, continued to take all the commandments of the *Torah* very seriously, yet it is remarkable to observe with what fluidity and discretion commandments such as this one were handled as time went on. Sanhedrin 8:1 retained the commandment for dealing with a rebellious son, but qualified it by defining the legal procedure in a way that made it highly unlikely that such a case would ever result in the execution of such a child. Even within Palestine itself, culture had evidently changed sufficiently to make such a reinterpretation necessary.

Something similar happened in the case of Egyptian religion. Again, let one example suffice. As every classicist knows, Hellenistic culture was extremely resistant to foreign influence. Movements from outside could take hold only if they adapted sufficiently to the indigenous culture of the Greco-Roman empire. When her cult was brought to the West, the Egyptian goddess Isis essentially became a Hellenistic deity. Even her temples and her statuary adopted the distinctively Greek style.

It would be difficult to exaggerate the significance of the fact that Christianity, although it had its origin on Palestinian soil, soon migrated to the West and became almost exclusively a western phenomenon.

Among the gospel writers it is Luke in particular who appears to have been concerned to present Christianity in a dress that was least likely to cause consternation to Theophilus, the representative of cultured Hellenism. For instance, Luke deliberately deleted from his sources any reference to the death of Jesus as a vicarious sacrifice. Although he followed Mark closely in other respects, it is instructive to note how he altered Mark 10:45 (see Luke 22:27) and Mark 14:24 (Luke 22:19b-20 is a later addition, as the NEB also recognizes).

The first and foremost champion of the Christian message in Hellenistic dress was Paul, the apostle to the Gentiles. Over against a party that insisted that Christianity was intrinsically tied to Jewish customs and culture, Paul adamantly maintained that Gentiles could be Christians without first becoming Jews. Gentiles could confess Christ as Lord just as Jews could. As a matter of fact, Paul found in Hellenistic culture certain traditions that allowed him to express Christian convictions in a way that was not possible in the Jewish milieu.

Again one example must suffice. The Old Testament, and Jewish culture as a whole, did not know of the practice of the adoption of sons. According to Hellenistic legal tradition, on the other hand, adoption was irreversible since it was a legal contract (see Gal. 3:15).

Whereas according to this tradition a naturally born son can be disinherited, an adopted son cannot. Here the social conventions of Hellenism provided Paul with a valuable tool to express the new relationship with God that Christians are privileged to enjoy.

In other respects, also, Paul was well-integrated into Hellenistic society. His attitude toward the state may serve as a case in point. While Revelation 13 captures the attitude of Jewish apocalypticism toward secular government when it portrays the secular authority as demonic, Paul represented the Hellenistic ideal. In his view all authority structures were instituted by God.

An investigation into the nature of New Testament ethics affords especially valuable insight into the problem of the relationship between faith and culture. It is striking to see in what pragmatic fashion the writers of the New Testament dealt with this subject. Particularly instructive is Paul's famous principle: although all things are lawful, certain ethical guidelines are laid down for the sake of good order and so as to promote undivided attention to the service of the Lord (see 1 Cor. 6:12; 7:35). Similarly, 1 Peter 2:12 introduces community regulations with the following admonition: "Maintain good conduct among the Gentiles, so that in case they speak against you as wrongdoers, they may see your good deeds and glorify God on the day of visitation."

The use of such community regulations was a characteristic feature of Hellenistic tradition, and the content of these New Testament lists does not materially differ from the norms of Hellenistic ethics. In the Deutero-Pauline Epistles and in later Christian literature, the virtues that are held up as ideals are practically identical with those of Hellenistic society generally. It appears that these lists of virtues and vices were simply taken over from Hellenistic culture in order to ensure that the Christian congregation would enjoy a good reputation among the townspeople (at least, 1 Peter 2:12 suggests that as the motivation).

The ethical guidelines were evidently derived from various sources. Only a few of these ethical norms can be shown to have emanated from the teaching of Jesus. In all probability Jesus had said little about the subject. When early Christians needed moral guidance, they seem to have relied mostly on Jewish and Hellenistic popular ethics and on common sense, which itself is always culturally conditioned.

For the most part, Paul was content to tolerate the cultural customs relating to food and drink, the keeping of holy days, the institution of slavery, and the submission to political authorities. In matters of sex, also, the early Christians, including Paul, appear to have been guided by the norms of the society around them.

The ethical counsels that we do find can hardly be considered as regulations for developing a distinctively Christian life-style. Rather, they appear to represent accommodations to, or simply adoptions of, the cultural ethic of the day and society. They are practical advice to live peaceably in society and to respect the norms that exist and are approved by all.

How far some segments of early Christianity were willing to go in their accommodation of the Christian tradition to the philosophical and religious presuppositions of their culture is illustrated by the fact that the entire tractate *Eugnostos the Blessed* was only superficially revised and attributed to Jesus by the adherents of a gnostic sect, remnants of whose literature were discovered at Nag Hammadi.

The gnostic branch was not, of course, the main branch of the Christian church, but every student of patristics cannot help but be amazed at the degree to which even the orthodox church Fathers interpreted the biblical text by reading into it the philosophical presuppositions of Hellenism.

This Hellenistic philosophy was essentially concerned with the "substance" or "essence" of things, a concept that is foreign to Jewish thought. Little wonder that soon the chief topic of discussion in the church became the question whether the substance of Jesus was identical with (*homoousios*) or similar to (*homoiousios*) the substance of the Father. The Nicene Creed recorded the victory of the former of these two positions when it included the phrase "of one substance with the Father."

What is notable here is simply this: the whole question had been occasioned by the necessity of defining the faith in contemporary categories of thought. In this connection it is worth pointing out that the more recent version of the Nicene Creed reads "of one Being with the Father." Evidently the "substance" formulation presents its own problems in a scientifically oriented society that analyzes and synthesizes substances.

Every creed and every formulation of the faith is in some important respects a product of the cultural milieu in which it was fashioned.

To say this is not to impugn the creeds or formulations of Christendom. It is to recognize that integral to the Christian articulation of the faith is the conviction that not all truth is located in the past, but that the present cultural milieu has a vital contribution to make in the discovery of how the Christian faith should be appropriately expressed *now*.

Faith and Culture in Dialectic Tension

We are faced with an intricate interplay between faith and culture. The relationship between the two is very difficult to unravel. In the discovery and proclamation of Christian truth, have our ancestors in the faith taken their cue from culture or from Christ? To put it another way, does culture serve as the lens through which one views Christ, or does Christ stand above culture as its judge? Does one's culture shape one's faith or does one's faith shape one's culture?

The answer must probably always remain ambivalent. To go too far in either direction would have serious consequences. If one interprets Christ wholly in terms of one's culture, as the gnostics did, then culture becomes the basic determinant, so that the object of one's contemplation is quite irrelevant. Then there is no appreciable difference between the faith that looks to Jesus the Christ and the faith that focuses on Eugnostos the Blessed, whoever he may be.

On the other hand, one must also acknowledge that it is naive to think that with our inevitably culturally conditioned vision we can apprehend a Christ who is totally other and stands above culture in an absolute way.

This much ought to be clear, however: we must not identify faith with culture in such a way that to believe means to adopt the cultural viewpoint of the people who formulated the faith, in whatever age. It is necessary to distinguish clearly between believing in the Christ and, for instance, believing that the earth is flat.

Christians in the 20th century should not be asked to practice medicine or to do science or to construct their cosmology in the way in which this was done in the first century. They may not even have to share the demonology or the angelology that was taken for granted then, and they are certainly free to develop new forms of worship that are more in touch with the way in which they now perceive God's creation and their life in the world.

Although the inspired authors of the New Testament writings accepted without question the economic institution of slavery and the social institution of the patriarchal family, as well as the cosmological concept of a two-tiered universe, it does not necessarily follow that contemporary Christians must do the same. Rather, if it is true that the early Christians largely respected the convention of their society in these matters, it may be defensible for the Christian community in the 20th century to be similarly in tune with contemporary mores of their own time and place.

Such a conclusion, however, can never be one with which to rest easy. We can never forget that although they used language that by its very nature was culturally conditioned, our Christian ancestors tended to transform that language when they employed it to speak of their faith and their God. The term *kyrios* may mean in Greek no more than "mister," or "sir," but when believers applied that term to Christ, the word assumed fundamentally new dimensions. Similarly, they transformed such common Greek words as *logos* and *ekklesia,* and a host of other terms. No doubt Paul was well aware that even the Hellenistic concept of the adoption of sons was far from adequate to express all there was to be said about the new relationship that pertained to Christians in the household of God. Although God speaks through culture, culture cannot contain God.

Two centuries after Paul, Origen knew that when human language is employed to speak of God and of divine matters generally, it can function only in an allegorical or in an approximate sense. If we describe God as father or mother, we do so in full recognition that God must be very much *un*like any human parent with whom we come into contact.

We cannot speak of God except in terms of our own cultural experience, yet we confess a God who bursts out of, and far transcends any cultural categories we may use. To the extent, however, that God does transcend our culturally limited frame of reference, God frustrates our ability to know and to understand. When this happens, we can speak only in hope and by faith, which reaches out beyond itself. Then we may need Kierkegaardian symbols, such as the concept of launching out on a deep sea or the figure of a trusting leap of faith into a dark void. When we speak in such terms, have we then finally escaped the strictures of culture altogether, or have we only exchanged the terms of a Hellenistic "substance" philosophy for the categories of existentialism—all of them equally culturally conditioned?

Implications for Christian Education

As we have seen, the Christian message has always been understood as a message for today. The good news is heard as a story from the past, but in every generation Christians have translated it into the categories of their own culture. Truth evidently does not belong exclusively to any culture, past or present. In every culture the gospel must be proclaimed in terms that are meaningful at the time. When artists like Dürer and Rembrandt represented the birth of Christ in a German stable or a Dutch farmhouse, they demonstrated that truth needs to be reformulated in every new day.

Faith does not require us to adopt the cultural presuppositions of 2000 years ago. It is not necessary for us to subscribe to the proposition, ". . . without the shedding of blood there is no forgiveness" (Heb. 9:22). What the author of this statement really wished to assert can be simply stated: "In Christ we experience a release that ultimately defies description in *any* category of human thought."

Can we learn to articulate the faith in symbols that are congenial to our contemporary culture? This is the challenge before us.

This essay is not a plea to make the faith *conform* to the demands of 20th-century scientific thought. The Christian faith inevitably demands a certain sacrifice of the human intellect. After all, we trust a God who brings life out of death. We follow a Christ who is a stumbling block for Jews and Greeks alike. Let us not, however, create artificial stumbling blocks by demanding that Christians today believe, as the ancients did, that the sun or stars can move and stop and move again. The offense of faith surely issues from another source, from a Savior who offers a cross and bids his followers to deny themselves and reach out to others in love.

It follows that Christian education is not essentially a matter of learning facts or of inculcating moral aphorisms. It is a process of stimulating the Christian community to find ways of living and acting that are appropriate in the sociocultural context in which this community is located.

Christian education is therefore to be regarded as a community enterprise. Even if the learning process takes place in the context of a teacher-student relationship, it is much more than a transmission of facts. It is more appropriate to think of it as the formation of a new consensus. What the "teacher" presents is, or at least intends to be, a *consensus fidelium,* and this consensus is being presented so that the group may consider it and form its own consensus in the process.

Since culture is always changing, the educational task can never be completed. On this side of eternity the answers can never be definitive. This insight, too, should leave an indelible imprint on the syllabus of any Christian course of study in seminary or parish.

Uniformity of conclusions is not to be expected, nor is it desirable. In a sociocultural context characterized by pluralism and change, universal answers would not be helpful, even if they were available. The Bible itself does not present a single cosmology, ethic, eschatology, or Christology. This, too, has something to say about the content, style, and objective of Christian education.

It does not follow, of course, that one position is as good as another. There are parameters. What these parameters are, however, cannot be stated in any precise fashion. We live not by law, but by grace.

SIX

EDUCATION FOR EVANGELIZATION

Donald L. Deffner

The focus of this chapter is on the mission and call of the church to share the good news with and within the world. "Education" for evangelization does not imply strategies, programs, or methods. Rather, it is a *habitus,* an understanding, a perspective with which to approach the joyous task of evangelization. This habitus is central to the educational task in Christian living. Evangelization by definition is the activity of bringing the gospel of salvation in Jesus Christ to people everywhere.

Religion in American Life

A January 1986, Gallup poll reports that little change has taken place in recent years in religion's effect on society. Fifty-five percent of the people interviewed said religion is very important in their lives. Ninety-one percent of Americans currently state a religious preference. Sixty-eight percent say they are members of a church or synagogue, and 42 percent of them go to worship weekly.

In an earlier study, *The Unchurched American,* George Gallup in connection with the Princeton Research Center found that 41 percent of the United States' population had no church connection.[1] That is not to say that all people inside churches are true believers, nor that nobody outside the church is a Christian. But it is still important to know why these people do not choose church membership.

Most of these unchurched people said they believe in God. Forty-five percent said they pray every day. Sixty-four percent said they believe Jesus Christ "is God or the Son of God," and 68 percent believe in his resurrection. A high 77 percent said they had some kind of religious training during their childhood.

Of course, for these people to believe theoretically in God, Christ, and the Bible is one thing, but to believe strongly enough to do something about it is far different.

Why don't they come to church? Six out of ten say that "most churches . . . have lost the real spiritual part of religion." And about half agree that "most churches . . . today are not effective in helping people find meaning in life." Thirty-six percent said churches "are not warm and accepting of outsiders."

And yet over half (52 percent) of these people who had formerly been active in church said they could possibly see situations where they would once again become active members. In fact, some of the encouraging statistics were that 74 percent of the unchurched want their children to have religious instruction. This is indeed a challenge to Christian educators—not only to follow our Lord's call to "feed my sheep," but also to "feed my lambs."

But why are they still outside the church?

Who Are the Unchurched?

Who Are the Unchurched? is the title of a fascinating study by the Rev. J. Russell Hale, professor of church and society at the Lutheran Theological Seminary, Gettysburg, Pennsylvania.[2] Noting that 125 million people are on church rolls in the United States (1977), Hale sought to understand why some 80 million people prefer to stay outside the church. He spent a month in each of six "irreligious" counties and interviewed some 165 people. He came up with 12 categories to describe the motives for people who have not decided to "drop back in."

1. The *Anti-institutionalists*. These see the church as preoccupied with self-maintenance, and they object to its political nature. They see its emphasis on finances, buildings, and property.

2. The *Boxed-in* are the "constrained" (in doctrine or ethics), "thwarted," or "independent types."

3. The *Burned-out* are the "used" (exploited or manipulated) or those now "light travelers."

4. The *Cop-outs* were never really rooted in the church to begin with; they are either the "apathetic" or the "drifters."

5. The *Happy Hedonists* idolize leisure pursuits.

6. Most tragic are the *Locked-out*. The "rejected" see themselves as "not good enough" to measure up to the church's expectations of holiness or perfection. The "neglected"—the poor, ethnic minorities, and the aging—have been overlooked and disregarded. The "discriminated against" are more hostile, though, for they have been looked at and deliberately excluded.

7. The *Nomads* are the wanderers in our society. (Between 1950 and 1960, about 40 million Americans changed their home addresses at least once a year.)

8. The *Pilgrims* are on an ideological pilgrimage, like one 86-year-old gentleman in Florida who said he was "still waiting for all the facts to come in."

9. The largest group by far are the *Publicans,* who scorn what they regard as the self-righteousness and hypocrisy of churchgoers. They prefer to stay on the outside since "there are too many half-hearted on the inside."[3]

10. The *Scandalized* gag at the proliferation of groups of "true believers," each of which claims to have exclusive possession of the keys to the kingdom.

11. The *True Unbelievers* are the smallest group numerically: Atheists/Agnostics; Deists/Rationalists; Humanists/Secularists.

12. The *Uncertain* "just don't know."[4]

Hale spells out the church's need for "active listening" in seeking to reach these "outsiders." Although it may not always be the church's fault, he notes how we need to forego conceit and acknowledge our own sinfulness and say, in the words of a nun in Alabama, "We ask your forgiveness."

Why People Join the Church

A most helpful follow-up study is Edward A. Rauff's *Why People Join the Church.*[5] He lists a number of factors for persons returning to the church: the influence of Christian people, family relationships and responsibilities, the search for community, personal crisis, a feeling of emptiness, the end of rebellion, the journey toward truth, the response to evangelism, the reaction to guilt and fear, God's *kairos* (a fitting time), church visit, program, sacred art, the influence of pastors.

His conclusion is, "The people of the church or friends and relatives are the most frequent source of evangelization."[6]

Some people, of course, will come back to the church "on their own." A student of mine researched this informally by phoning 35 people who had joined a large San Francisco Bay Area church. The main reason these people came back was that "life was a drag." "There must be more to life than this dull routine," they said. So they tried the church again. Ninety percent had been very active in a youth group. They had dropped out at around age 18—when they felt there was nothing more for them.

But when they came back, the key was that they had been welcomed at the door by some members of the church, and within one week someone other than the pastor had called on them and in a relaxed way said, "We would be happy to share our church with you. How can we help you?"

This is similar to the comment of Rebecca Manley Pippert (associated with Inter-Varsity Christian Fellowship), who said she had talked with a minister who reported that his church had tried every kind of high-powered, structured outreach. After five years, only one person had come to his church as a result of all this strategy, and that new member came because he had established a friendship with a church member who had simply knocked on his door.

The result of that insight was that the pastor began training the congregation in how to lead effective neighborhood Bible studies, taught them principles of relational evangelism, and encouraged them to reach out to the people right where they lived.[7]

Our Approach

In the light of all this, what are the implications for our approach to the unchurched?

Leighton Ford, evangelist, stated:

• We should be expectant. Many non-Christians are open to dialog about religion.

• Realism dictates that the basic problem is still self-centeredness—an easy religion. "Like the Samaritan woman, they want living water, but they want a boyfriend, too."[8]

• Evangelism requires intense personal involvement.

• The church must incarnate forgiveness—not moralism or legalism. (To the charge that there are too many hypocrites in the church, we may quip: "Come on in. There's always room for one more." But often we *are* seen as duplicitous. What others outside the church are looking for, says Richard Quebedeaux, is "persistent exemplary behavior.")

• We need to confront a false individualism.

• We need to relate our teaching to life.

• We need to reach out, not just wait for them to come.

• We need to take time and show long-range concern. "Evangelism is a process and not just an experience or event."[9]

• Mass-media outreach to the unchurched needs to be related more to local churches.[10]

The Heart of Evangelism

And what is the heart of evangelism? Deane A. Kemper states: "The Great Awakenings, the revivals of the nineteenth century, the surge in Church membership that followed World War II, and the continuing growth of Christianity on university campuses stemmed not from grand designs, and expensive promotions, but from the work of the Holy Spirit in individual congregations, obscure pastors, small prayer meetings and local gatherings of concerned believers."[11]

So the focal point is *the local congregation.*

As Richard Lischer says in *Speaking of Jesus: Finding the Words for Witness:* "The matter of this book . . . will not deal with ecclesiastical policies for recouping losses nor with congregational strategies for growing big churches. This evangelism 'from above' threatens to take work away from those who had it from the beginning—the people of God." [12]

Lischer also aptly calls us to our Lord's own model for evangelization: (1) dialogic, (2) holistic, (3) situational, (4) using simple language, (5) decisive. [13]

What Then Is Our Task?

The Gospel

Our Lord's ultimate words to his disciples were: "the message about repentance *to* the forgiveness of sins. . ." (author's trans.). This must be preached "to all nations . . ." (Luke 24:46-49). According to the accepted Greek text, it is "repentance *to* "not "repentance *and.*" It is the preaching of the law *that there might be* conviction of sin and reception of the good news of the gospel.

This is also the message which is essential to Paul's declaration of the gospel (1 Corinthians 15; 2 Corinthians 5). It is the central core of the sermons in the book of Acts (see Acts 2:38; 3:19-20; 13:38-39; 15:9). Repentance *to* the forgiveness of sins is always the heart of the declaration—and is linked to the resurrection.

The Mission

The mission of the church is to announce the good news, irrespective of results. *Mission* therefore is not program, activity, methods, numbers, visible achievements, or strategy. It is what happens when lives that have been changed by the Holy Spirit come in contact with the contemporary world. Mission is not statistics but sacrifice. It means being poured out as a libation with a cost of discipleship that can lead to martyrdom.

The Mystery and the Hope

In reaching out
you are reached
In giving
you receive
In changing
you are changed
In loving
you are loved
In saving
you are saved
In serving
you are fulfilled
Christ in you—
the mystery
and
the hope
of
the
world[14]

Matthew 7:7-8; Colossians 1:27

Reaching the Educated

A special word needs to be said about the church's mission to the "educated" American. The "educated" are those with or without a college education who have grappled with the great ontological questions of life in depth. Though numerically fewer, these are the persons in America with influence—the power brokers, the symbol manipulators. "If the church fails to bring the Gospel to these people, it shall fail to speak to America itself," said Joel H. Nederhood in his classic text *The Church's Mission to the Educated American* (Eerdmans, 1960, p. 57).

A fine summation of our task for this dialog was produced by Rev. James Oldham in my Graduate Theological Union (Berkeley) course, "Reaching the Educated Adult."[15]

Common Characteristics of the Educated Adult	*Implications for the Church's Ministry of Evangelism & Education*
1. Have extensive vocabularies; possess higher than average verbal and quantitative abilities; prefer abstract to concrete thinking.	1. Present Christian faith option at a level commensurate with their academic achievement. Be prepared to deal with intellectual objections to faith, but also to interpret the nature of faith as a suprarational reality.
2. Tend to depend more on art, music, drama, literature, and other print media and less on popular mass media (radio, TV, movies) for their information and worldview.	2. Need to be well-acquainted with these sources so that we can understand the frame of reference from which the educated are coming.
3. Are well-acquainted with a broad spectrum of the liberal arts, including philosophy, history, psychology, sociology, literature, and current events; interdisciplinary in their thinking.	3. Stress the positive relationship between Christianity and these disciplines. Draw heavily on them for insights which undergird the Christian message and demonstrate the ways in which faith may impact on their teachings and practices.
4. Tend to view religious faith as irrelevant and otherworldly.	4. Emphasize the Christian faith as something relevant to every aspect of one's life and work and the concerns of today's society rather than a "Sunday only" or "heavenly only" type of reality. Use modern translations of Scripture, contemporary Christian writers, and nontraditional religious jargon in presentations and dialog.
5. Are philosophically committed to research, open discussion, and empirical experiences as the final validators of truth.	5. Avoid claiming revelation for something that is only speculation. Present beliefs of Christianity as tenets to be explored and investigated rather than closed issues. Challenge openness to the claims of Christ.

6. Are more open to diversity of thought and more able to stand outside themselves to see another perspective.

6. Present options for interpretation and alternatives for action rather than fixed answers, whenever possible. Encourage discussion, dialog, and debate as helpful methods of conversion and growth. Be nondefensive and nonthreatened.

7. Tend to be universalistic rather than particularistic in their views of religion and salvation.

7. Acknowledge genuine points of congruence between Christianity and other faiths. Tactfully point out meaningful differences. Stress potential negative impact of the universalist position.

8. Look to organizations and individuals to establish their authority through competence and moral suasion rather than authoritarian wielding of power or clever manipulation.

8. Deemphasize authoritarian attitudes and styles. Convey credibility through calm self-assurance, integrity, genuine compassion, and reliance on the Holy Spirit.

9. Tend to act more from esteem, actualization, and service needs than from safety or security needs.

9. Scratch where they itch—present claims of the gospel addressed to this orientation (e.g., rich young ruler). Emphasize the scattering as well as the gathering function of God's people.

10. Are highly self-directed in the process of learning.

10. Involve the educated themselves not only in learning experiences but also in the planning and evaluation of learning. Recognize the usefulness and effectiveness of more individualized settings and techniques of learning.

11. Prefer diversity and innovation in style and content of programming, services, learning experiences, etc.

11. Offer a variety of programs for the educated, tailored to their time schedules, life-styles, and learning preferences rather than expecting or requiring them to fit into the way "we've always done it."

12. Less tolerant of boring repetition, senseless get-togethers, and perceived busywork.

12. Quality must be emphasized in all aspects of programming and ministry, particularly the areas of leadership and resource development. Requests for time and talent involvement should relate to meaningful ministry, not routine or counterproductive institutional maintenance.

13. May have reservations (or even hostility) about the validity of the Christian faith, because their experience of it has been limited to very closed, judgmental, antiintellectual expressions.

13. Help educated to understand these expressions and the *Sitz im Leben* of those involved in them. Lift up true Christianity as broader, intellectually honest, and. more humane and liberating than these.

SEVEN

HUMAN DEVELOPMENT AND CHRISTIAN EDUCATION

Margaret A. Krych

Learning about and responding to the good news of God's mercy and forgiveness in Jesus Christ is a lifelong process. Children at their level of learning hear the Word and respond in their own ways; teenagers and adults hear and respond in their maturing ways. Never is the learning complete. Always there are new insights into God's grace and forgiveness in Jesus Christ for our redemption, into the privileges and responsibilities of membership in the church, and into the work of the Holy Spirit as the believer lives out his or her Baptism in daily life. Therefore, the church's educational ministry includes all age levels. We shall consider each of these broad groupings in this chapter.

Basic Developmental Considerations

Why consider human beings at all? Is not the content of the gospel that which is important in teaching? Certainly the content is central. But the gospel is the message of God's action on behalf of human beings, and it calls for a response of faith on the part of hearers. Paul Tillich has said that for the gospel to be truly heard, it is necessary to correlate the questions in the human situation with the answer of the

111

gospel.[1] In other words, we cannot simply proclaim good news without taking account of those to whom the news is proclaimed. The deep human needs answered in God's work in Christ must be brought to awareness so that the gospel is received as relevant. Another way that Christians have expressed this is to say that the law must be proclaimed together with the gospel. This might seem to be pure common sense. But it is surprising how often teachers fail to ask the simple but important question, How will my students most clearly hear and perceive the relevance of this message for themselves?

Biblical facts per se are not the focal point of Christian education. The focus must always be the gospel—the message of God's good news in Jesus Christ. Biblical stories will undoubtedly be used extensively and biblical passages explored carefully. And this must always be so, because the Bible is the primary written witness to the revelation of God in Christ. But the biblical material will always be explored in order that the hearer may respond to the message of the gospel.

An important factor in communicating the gospel is the nature of the learner. The old contrast between content-centered and learner-centered education is a false dichotomy in Christian teaching. The content of the gospel is crucial; but so is the learner who hears and responds. To ignore either is to fail to communicate the Christian message. Tillich suggests that we must seek to participate in the learner's situation in order to present the gospel in a way that is relevant.[2] Information about the human beings who learn must be taken very seriously by those of us who teach. Of course, some information about our students will be more pertinent than will other facts. But we must ask of any information, Does this have a bearing on the way my students think, feel, and behave? How can this help me in communicating the gospel to them?

Developmental theory gives us a growing body of information about persons of all age levels. In dealing with human beings, the teacher of adults needs to know about children and youth. In order to understand adult learners, it is helpful to grasp the developmental journey they have already made. Conversely, teachers of children will have broader vision if they grasp the developmental journey and the learning that lie ahead of their students during adolescence and adulthood. Christian educators need to consider carefully such information in preparing to teach. In dealing with human development, we are, of course, dealing with an aspect of God's creation.

All aspects of a human being are relevant to the educator. Jesus ministered to the whole person; in dealing with physical and emotional needs, he also ministered spiritually. In educational ministry we also must deal with the whole learner—socially, emotionally, intellectually, physically, and spiritually. On a purely pragmatic level, educators have long known that all aspects of the learner affect learning. Susan will not retain cognitive information if she is emotionally torn over her parents' announcement that they are getting a divorce. John will be unable to concentrate on his work if he has a fever. Physiological readiness can make a task virtually impossible for three-year-old Edward, boringly simple for 12-year-old Petra, but exciting and challenging for eight-year-old Adam.

In this chapter it will be impossible to draw implications for religious education from every social, emotional, intellectual, physical, and spiritual characteristic of learners. Therefore, some examples will be given from each broad age-grouping to indicate the way in which information on human development can be used to facilitate learning, develop suitable procedures, choose appropriate content, and the like. But they will be examples only. It will be for the reader to explore the ever-growing fund of information from psychology, sociology, and pastoral care, and to consider their relevance in teaching the gospel.

The following sections include many generalizations. Statistical "norms" are helpful in telling us what is generally likely to be true of an age level, but each person is an individual and will vary more or less from these "normal" patterns. Endeavor to learn the characteristics of individual students so that you are able to modify age-level expectations accordingly. Learn, too, cultural and ethnic information that may be pertinent in dealing with your students

Cognitive Development and Religious Education

In teaching the gospel, it is necessary to balance cognitive information with emotional and social learning. The cognitive dimension (how people think) is certainly not more important than other aspects of the learner. However, a separate section on cognitive development and its implications for Christian education is warranted for two reasons: first, because of the tremendous impact of research in cognitive development on religious education in the last couple of decades, and second, because the age stages in cognitive development cut across the usual categories of preschool, elementary years, and adolescence, which will be used in the remainder of the chapter.

Research in cognitive development, especially since the early 1960s, has revolutionized religious education. No longer do we think of children as miniature adults, but instead we recognize that the thinking of children is qualitatively different from that of adults. Moreover, there are stages of thinking within childhood itself. We have found that we must teach less content much more thoroughly to children, and more content in greater depth to teenagers and adults.

A brief overview of the different stages of thinking will help to illustrate implications for religious education. We shall use the developmental stages of Jean Piaget, a giant in the field of cognitive development, whose stages have been substantiated by researchers on various continents with persons of many socioeconomic and educational backgrounds. Piaget posited six stages in cognitive development, which are the result of maturation and hold true for all children.[3] The ages at which the stages appear depend on inherited factors and also on the environment in which the child is reared.[4] The first three stages (sometimes considered as one) last until about two years of age. Stages four, five, and six, particularly, concern the parish educator, because children usually begin formal church education at about three years of age. So we shall examine these latter stages of preoperational, concrete, and abstract thinking.

Crucial to Piaget's scheme are the processes of *assimilation, accommodation, substitution,* and *integration. Assimilation* is the process by which new items are assimilated into an existing scheme (when Alice first sees a cow, she calls it a large cat). *Accommodation* changes existing schemes to fit new events (the cow moos, and Alice decides it cannot be a cat and asks her father what it is). *Substitution* occurs when the child replaces a less mature idea with a more mature one. For this to happen, the child must be mentally ready for the new concept. *Integration* is the process of bringing together less mature ideas into more complex conceptions. It also presupposes readiness to move forward.

The notion of readiness is important for those of us who teach. Rather than attempting to drive information into the child as early as possible, it is easier and far more pleasant for both student and teacher to wait until the child is ready for particular concepts. When her teacher capitalizes on readiness, Alice will learn eagerly and with a sense of accomplishment.

Preoperational thinking

The stage of *preoperational thinking* lasts from approximately two to seven years of age. It includes the two substages of *preconceptual thought* (two to four years) and *intuitive thought* (four to seven years).

From two to four years, children develop the use of words as symbols, develop memory of the past, and begin to make believe. Their thought is often distorted by trying to fit reality to their own desires and is characterized by egocentricity. (This is not to be confused with the theological use of egocentricity as sin—equally characteristic of all persons of all ages.) Cognitive egocentricity is the inability to take another person's viewpoint due to intellectual immaturity. For example, it is inappropriate to say to three-year-old John, "Think how Jennifer feels when you shout at her," because John literally is incapable of imagining how Jennifer feels. He can see the world only from his own point of view. Appropriate learnings for egocentric Threes and Fours are, "God loves *me*," "*I* can thank God," "God loves *my* family."

A further characteristic of preoperational thought is *transductive reasoning*—that is, reasoning from particular to particular (not from particular to general and vice versa, as adults do). Such reasoning assumes relationships that do not exist, and teachers are often amused, surprised, or confused at the child's reasoning.

Intuitive thought continues to lack logic. The child centers or focuses on part of a problem and ignores other parts or the relation of parts to the whole. This is called *centration*. Intuitive thought also lacks *reversibility*—the process by which we check the accuracy of our thinking. Young children often make strange assumptions about God, Jesus, the Bible. Unable to check their reasoning logically, children may hold a variety of irreconcilable notions simultaneously. It is, therefore, important to teach just a few concepts clearly, using straightforward and brief sentences, and repeating often.

Young children often use words before knowing their meaning. And, conversely, they may have concepts that they cannot express because they do not have appropriate vocabulary. Help children build vocabulary when necessary. Endeavor to use the simplest, clearest words to say what you mean. And take time to let the children express their ideas.

Preoperational thinkers do not distinguish between fact and fantasy. Well-meaning teachers may attempt to distinguish between those persons who are real (God, Jesus) and things that are fantasy (Santa Claus, Easter Bunny). This distinction will be appropriate and even essential after the age of seven. But it means little to preschoolers, because concepts of fact and fantasy are simply beyond them.

Concepts of time and space are not yet developed. Therefore historical and geographical references are merely confusing and should be avoided. More helpful are vague terms such as "long ago" and "far away." And be prepared for the children to believe that Moses, Jesus, grandpa, and even you as a child were all contemporaries!

In preoperational thinking, *wrong* is conceived not in terms of intentionality but in terms of amount of damage done and that for which one is punished. Nor are children able to reason from principles to particular instances. Therefore, they do not engage in ethical reasoning.

Preoperational children think of God as having a physical body. Since children cannot think in any other way, the wise teacher will not attempt to teach God as spirit or focus on omnipresence, but will focus on the characteristics of God that are consistent with the biblical message of the gospel and are related to experiences the child may grasp—God is caring, loving, someone to be trusted, someone whose promises are true, who can be praised and thanked, who is interested in the individual child. A few simple concepts about God, Jesus, and the church are sufficient and should be reviewed often. Young children love to hear their favorite stories again and again. The children will learn more conceptual material as they grow older. Meanwhile, if the children are limited in reasoning ability, they are wide open to wonder and awe and thanksgiving, which can be used extensively in teaching.

Concrete operations

At about seven years of age, the brain cells will have matured to the point where a new kind of thinking is possible. The period of *concrete operations* lasts from 7 to 11 or 12 years of age. The child is now able to use logical operations due to decentration and reversibility—that is, the child can focus on the interrelation of wholes and parts and can reason about the reverse of procedures and so check arguments. However, the child is still limited to thinking about that which in principle can be perceived through the senses—that is, about things which, in principle can be touched, tasted, smelled, seen, or heard. The child continues to conceive of God as having a physical body somewhere (whether of human shape that invisibly darts around the world like Superman or of some other beautiful color and shape). Concepts of spirit, Trinity, and so on are beyond concrete thinkers.

During this period there is growth in the ability to generalize. To aid comprehension of generalizations, give plenty of examples. Rather than saying, "Remember to love everyone," begin with specifics. "Here are some ways of showing love to your sister and grandfather. Now, tell me some ways you can show love to your friends at recess. There are ways to be loving to everyone."

Similarly, concrete thinkers are able to see the point of view of others but will appreciate repetition of the steps in such reasoning. "When someone yells at you, how do you feel? When you yell at Bobby, do you think he feels the same way you do when someone yells at you? The things that you don't like done to you are likely the things that Bobby won't like. And the things you do like may well be things he likes. We try to do things for others that they will like and avoid doing things they won't like."

A child can grasp simple concrete simile (how an orange and the sun are alike). But metaphors in which similarity does not depend on obvious sensory characteristics are beyond them. Taken literally by the child, such metaphors may be misconstrued. Metaphors like "Rock of Ages" or "door of the sheep" are better left until after age 12 when, in the next stage of thinking, they will mean a great deal. Most parables, also, are better left until the abstract thinking stage. A straightforward story such as the good Samaritan, in which the hearer is bidden to help someone in need, is easily grasped by a concrete thinking child. But parables with typical "hidden meaning" require metaphorical thinking (the kingdom of heaven is like a mustard seed; the lost coin; and so on). Using these wonderful stories too soon can blunt the excitement of appreciating the hidden meaning when the student becomes old enough to understand them.

From ages 7 to 12, the child develops concepts of time, space, speed, and causality. It is appropriate to introduce biblical history and geography with maps from about third or fourth grade.

By nine or ten years the child begins to take account of intention in judging moral right and wrong, develop genuine ethical concepts, and grasp broken relationships and forgiveness in a mature way. This is an excellent time to point to God, who forgives in spite of what we are like and what we have done. Children may be prepared for their first Communion at this age, with an emphasis on forgiveness. At the same time, the older elementary child forms strong concepts of justice and fairness, and finds grace a difficult notion to grasp. Specially structured narratives may help in communicating acceptance through grace.[5]

It is not until the beginning of the concrete stage that children grasp that everyone will die. And even at fourth grade, less than 50 percent of children may understand that death is irrevocable and the cessation of corporeal life.[6] Death, resurrection, and Easter may be very profound and moving for some students, while others may honestly wonder what all the fuss is about. Some may even wonder only that it took Jesus so long to come back to life!

During the concrete stage, fact is separated from fantasy. Children need your help in pointing out those figures that are fantastic (Santa) and those that are real (God, Jesus).

Concrete thinkers will grasp a good many biblical insights and parts of some doctrines. As early as first grade, for example, Baptism may be presented as a special way of saying that God loves this person and that the person becomes part of God's people, the church. Holy Communion may be introduced to second graders as a special time when we thank God for his love, remember Jesus, and are with God and people who love him; about the age of ten, the understanding of forgiveness can be added. In addition to what they grasp, many aspects of faith will be apprehended rather than comprehended—the children will have a genuine awareness, often through experienced attitudes and behaviors, which they may not be able to express or even to recognize when described by adults. And there will also be many parts of the Bible and theological formulations that will be totally beyond them.

Always distinguish the difficulty of a concept from the deceptively simple words in which it may be couched. For example, "Jesus died for your sins on the cross" uses simple words, but the concept of vicarious suffering on behalf of sinners is a very complex one. Teachers and pastors need to practice the difficult art of thinking concretely in order to communicate with the child. Learning to speak in concrete terms and knowing what to omit takes practice, thought, time, and care.

Abstract thinking

About the age of 11 or 12, a child reaches the stage of *abstract thinking* or formal operations. There are no further stages; this is the kind of thinking that adults use the world over. The person who engages in abstract thinking deals with general ideas and abstract constructions, uses combinatorial logic[7] and symbols for symbols,[8] is able to construct ideals, reasons about the future, introspect, apply principles in theory, use metaphor, grasp universal generalizations, reason about that which is contrary to fact,[9] and is no longer limited to thinking about that which is perceivable in principle through the senses.

The Bible is full of abstract concepts. Consider the prophetic literature, the teachings of Jesus, and Paul's letters. Christian theology, catechisms, creeds—all assume the ability to use formal operations. Since the adolescent is ready to "put together" on a cognitive level the whole Christian message for the first time, this age level is one of the most exciting to teach. The deep faith of childhood now has the added dimension of fuller understanding and grasp of traditional modes of expression. Often the adolescent experiences a deeper personal response to Jesus Christ and a desire to share the good news as this new dimension is added.

Much theological thinking is quite complex. It first requires practice in general abstract thinking, then requires sensitive teachers who are able to explain theological terms simply, use metaphor and parable regularly, teach from that which is known to that which is unknown, review constantly, and understand the need for adolescents frequently to return to the easier mode of concrete thinking. Cognitively, early teenagers are like toddlers learning to walk: they stumble, practice, are proud of their attempts, and need the support of caring adults. In teaching adolescents, first learn as much as you can about the Christian faith. Then put theological terms into your own words. Next, analyze each doctrine (God, sin, Christ, justification, and so on) into those aspects that are simplest and most likely to be grasped at the end of the concrete thinking stage. Begin teaching these concepts and then gradually move on to the more difficult ones.[10]

Implications for Christian Education

In general, age-stage theory has many implications for Christian education. We must teach much less content more thoroughly at younger age levels, and we need to be aware that young children do not merely store away phrases they do not understand, but rather assimilate them to what they already know, which results in misconceptions that may later need to be unlearned. We must avoid mistaking parroting of words for genuine understanding and be alert to metaphorical statements that children will take literally. Above all, we must learn to appreciate all stages of thinking and respect them. Never laugh at children's efforts to make sense of what they have heard. Work with children's thinking to develop a view of God consistent with the gospel that makes sense at the children's level. Keep in mind that the educational enterprise is a team effort: your teaching builds on that which others have taught, and others in turn will build on that which you teach. None of us has to teach the entire Bible to students in any one year! And always remember that the child's value in God's sight depends on God's own love and initiative in claiming the child in Christ, not on the child's ability to reason cognitively about beliefs.

In using the Bible, sometimes you will want to paraphrase with young children, and sometimes you will present the meaning of a passage without using the actual passage. For example, rather than tell the parable of the prodigal son to children, it is better to use straightforward statements. For four-year-olds, this might be, "God loves us even when we do things that make him sad." For ten-year-olds it might be, "God loves and forgives each of us." However, in early teens you will use the parable and help the students slowly "unpack" its meaning. With adults, you might simply tell the parable.

Sometimes curricula promise that all ages will study the same passages on a given day. By now it should be clear that such a promise is inappropriate. There will indeed be a small number of passages that can be used with all age levels. But selection of biblical texts for children must be chosen with care, and many passages are better left for later years.

One of the clearest implications of age-stage theory is the enormous educational task and great opportunities in adolescence and adulthood for building on early learnings and presenting the Christian faith in a whole and integrated fashion. While not neglecting to teach children, parishes must also endeavor to engage all teenagers and adults in a variety of solid educational experiences. Since many persons are afraid to teach teenagers and adults, there is a need to train persons to lead groups and use materials that encourage group members to be active participants in learning.

Many adults continue to use concrete thinking in regard to religious beliefs, although they use abstract thinking in most areas of their lives. Having left Sunday school about the age of 11, they have not had practice in thinking through their beliefs in a mature way. The wise teacher of adults will seek to "unpack" metaphor, define theological terminology, and help learners rephrase beliefs in their own words. There will be some adults who will operate for longer (through mental impairment) or shorter (through trauma) periods in the concrete thinking mode. Teachers need to know when to communicate the gospel in the concrete, using experiences and illustrations suited to adults.[11]

Children

In the interest of simplicity, we shall divide childhood into the period between birth and the beginning of church school, preschool (ages three to five or the completion of kindergarten), and the elementary years (grades one through six).

Birth to the beginning of church school

From birth to the beginning of church school is a period of great growth and learning. Physically, children acquire basic skills in locomotion, perception, and manipulation. During church services, a good, safe, warm, spacious "nursery" enables children to practice touching, toddling, and talking while experiencing the church buildings as a safe and pleasant environment. An environment that may be explored safely through manipulation avoids the necessity of saying, "Don't touch"—a signal that, when often repeated, conveys to the child that the church is a fearful and frustrating place to be.

Mentally, the child has developed ideas (concepts) before being able to express them verbally. Young children use single words for sentences, resulting in frustration for adults who fail to understand and for the child who is not understood. Acquisition of speech is aided by talking *to* very small children and not over their heads to their parents. In caring for small children, support verbalization of love and care with appropriate gestures and behavior.

Emotionally, the very young child exhibits whole-person responses. Peter is totally angry; Juanita is completely joyous. Emotions are intense but short-lived. Reasoning with a child in a tantrum is rarely successful; a firm, loving hug that restrains the child is more useful in preventing harm while communicating love. Since tiny children are often afraid of strangers, it is helpful to assign only one or two loving persons to greet each child regularly. A crowd of people or a rotation of strange faces may communicate that the church is a fearsome community.

If small children are present in the worship service, remember that loud singing, bells, and other loud noises can be frightening. On the other hand, gentle sounds, the warmth and security of the family, and a variety of interesting textures will help make the service a warm and loving experience.

Socially, the family is the most important factor in the life of a young believer. Peers are relatively unimportant to the toddler, except as nuisances who interfere with one's toys or as themselves intriguing "toys" to stare at and poke! Too often we think of Christian education as something that begins with a formal program on the church premises.

But some of the most important learning takes place much earlier. The confirming of an individual's faith begins at Baptism. The earliest Christian educators are parents, and a congregation that works with parents to prepare them for this valuable task is engaged in preparing educators who share the gospel by voice, touch, attitude, love, trustworthiness, and security long before the child can recognize the word *God*. In order for the child later to learn about and believe in God, who loves unconditionally, the child needs early experiences that help to make sense of acceptance and love. It is in the home that the first experiences of love and trust are given, and parents lay the foundational learnings of the gospel. (Here the term *parent* means any person who fulfills the parental role, whether biological parent, guardian, grandparent, etc.; *home* refers to the primary residential environment, whether family apartment or institutional group home.) The child who lacks a predictable, secure, loving, and trustworthy environment will later find difficulty in comprehending a God pictured in the Bible as trustworthy, faithful, loving, and merciful. In the home the child can experience a quality of life motivated by the Christian faith and grounded in the forgiveness of God. The Holy Spirit surely works in the life of small believers through the church and through the parents as the child's major experience of the church.

If the gospel is to be communicated, parents must spend time with their offspring. We need to reconsider the tendency to involve young parents on councils and committees to "keep them interested." Some may be able to serve on committees, but many working parents will not be able to give time to both church committees and children. As *the* Christian educators of their toddlers, parents have important work in the family that takes precedence over committee assignments. Their expertise will still be available to the congregation in years to come!

Many parents need support for particular reasons—the parent who feels trapped in childrearing, the single parent, the parent who is jealous of the new baby, the step-family, the working parent who feels guilty for spending so little time with the child. Helping the parent feel more comfortable will increase the chances of secure and loving care for the child. The congregation can offer support and provide groups to share experiences. A congregation that ignores young families fails to take seriously its baptismal responsibilities.

Preschool

In the preschool stage children show further physical development in basic skills of movement, perception, and manipulation. In this period of large-muscle activity, children are restless and energetic. It is difficult to overemphasize the importance of adequate space for children to move, run, jump, and play games and of furnishings that are the correct height. Preliminary small-muscle activity begins about four years of age; cutting, pasting, drawing, and (later) printing are clumsy at first. Children need large sheets of paper, fat crayons, large brushes, and plenty of extras to throw away when they "mess up." Parishes can expect that furnishings and materials will cost more in the preschool classes, and they should avoid buying small crayons and other inappropriate materials just because they are on sale. Incidentally, correct size of furniture, cleanliness, and safety do not mean that every item must be brand-new or expensive. Ingenuity and second-hand equipment often produce excellent quality of education on a limited budget.

Preschoolers learn through doing, not having someone do things for them. Shannon will learn far more by making her own cross-eyed puppet with straggly hair than by assembling a prepackaged item made by adults. She needs to experiment and make things for herself. In this way she practices small-muscle coordination, reinforces learning, and develops a sense of accomplishment and self-worth. Process rather than end product is what is important.

Since making things, painting, pasting, cooking, and water play are excellent but messy activities, try to locate preschool space near kitchen and bathrooms.

Mentally, preschoolers are in the preoperational stage described above. They have a short attention span, so limit oral presentation and storytelling to one minute per year of age (three minutes for three-year-olds, and so on). Since such limitation is difficult, try timing yourself before class.

Preschoolers have only very rudimentary concepts of time (today, yesterday, tomorrow, and sometimes the days of the week—often in the wrong order!). In some areas, such as time and money, preschoolers have only very rudimentary concepts. Stewardship education is therefore not appropriate for young children. And stories can profitably be told without historical settings.

Since young children have no understanding of intrinsic right and wrong, guide behavior simply by making a few clear rules: "Here we don't hit. Here we don't kick. Here we don't run." You will need to give frequent reminders as children forget quickly in the heat of an argument over clay or dolls.

Suitable concepts for preschoolers include: this is God's world; we can thank God for the world; Jesus was a wonderful man; God loves and cares about *me;* God loves my family; people in the church love me; we can help each other at home and at church school; God cares about me even when grown-ups or children are angry or mean.

The small child lives in a world of law, of dos and don'ts. Fear of a God who punishes and condemns is not uncommon. Therefore it is important to emphasize the gospel. The law can drive to Christ only when we already have some notion of God's mercy in Christ. Constantly point to God's love, relating this good news to the child's experiences. Children need particular assurance that God still cares, even when we make him sad or when adults are angry.

Beware of stories that can easily be misconstrued, such as Daniel (look what happens to people who pray—they get thrown in the lion's den!). Always ask, Will the story communicate to the child the good news of God's love and mercy revealed in Jesus Christ? The story of Noah, for example, may well do that for an adult who understands the notion of covenant, but to a small child, the narrative may more appropriately convey a God who drowned people and animals because he was angry.

Stories in the Bible suitable for young children include stories of Jesus who cared about people and helped them; nativity stories; what it was like when Jesus was a child; stories about friends (such as David and Jonathan), families (Ruth and Naomi), and God's care in difficult situations (Abraham's long journey, Moses' fear of a difficult task).

Socially, the preschool years are a time of imitation. It is probably more important for the child to see beloved adults praying at home and attending worship than it is to be taught rote prayers. The family remains the most important social group for the child, although peers gradually assume greater significance with the formation of same-sex friends by about six years of age. In choosing stories, remember the value of a secure family environment for the child. Threatening stories include those of Samuel, whose mother gave her child to a strange "minister" and left him at the "church"; Moses, whose mother left him floating in a river with only a sister to take care of him; and Joseph, whose jealous brothers dropped him in a pit! Traditional adult favorites are not necessarily appropriate for small children.

When the child begins Sunday school, encourage parents to stay until the child feels comfortable and is ready to stay in the new surroundings. This may take a few minutes, an entire session, or even portions of several sessions. This will help the child develop positive feelings about the church from the outset.

Young children demand a great deal of adult attention. The highest ratio of teachers to pupils should be in preschool classes, because children need individual interest and encouragement. Praise generously. In the earliest stages of self-evaluation, children have little experience of their capabilities and cannot slough off negative criticism easily, nor readily assess their efforts. Therefore, critique sparingly and look for the positive. You might say, "I'm so glad that you have worked so hard, David. What lovely colors! Tell me about it." Do not say, "Whatever is it? Here, let me show you the right way."

Preschoolers are learning social skills such as helping and taking turns. They need your guidance in practicing these skills. Free play provides rich opportunities for learning social skills and taking roles. To ensure maximum value in free play, watch for opportunities to label and praise helpful behavior, like, "It was nice of you, Sam, to give the car to Sara. That was a friendly thing to do."

Preschoolers need security of routine and familiar people. At least some of the teachers should be willing to commit themselves for the entire year. The class schedule should follow the same broad pattern every time, although story content and activities will differ. Above all, in the classroom as at home, children should experience love and acceptance through words, touch, and attitude. In correcting behavior, it is helpful to give a hug or verbal assurance that you love the child, even though you do not want the particular behavior repeated. In this way the child can gain some appreciation of acceptance in spite of that which is unacceptable—which, after all, is the essence of God's attitude to sinful humanity.

Encourage congregational members to express interest in preschoolers by speaking to them directly. Be sure there is at least one mature adult in the "nursery" to care for young children; egocentric children need other-centered persons to show patience and care, and young teens who are themselves focused on self find it difficult to give such care consistently. If children attend church, pastors who greet parishioners at the door should always shake the proffered hand (often the left!) of small children, just as with adults.

Elementary years

The elementary years are typified by marked changes in appearance and abilities. Many parts of the body mature or approach maturity. These years are invaluable for developing an appreciation of and respect for the body as part of God's wonderful world. The children have boundless physical energy. If there is no space for physical activity in the classroom, take the children outdoors when weather permits. Elementary children develop and refine both large- and small-muscle skills that can be used in learning. In the early grades, correct size of furniture is crucial for writing and drawing; no child can write well with legs swinging and arms stretched up to adult-size tables. In the later grades children may be comfortable on full-size furniture.

Mentally, elementary children move into the concrete thinking stage at about seven years of age (see above for characteristics of their thinking). If you combine grades one and two, some children will still be in the preoperational stage, while others will be in the concrete stage. By phrasing questions and stories to suit the younger members of the class, you will avoid the danger of the concrete thinkers laughing at less mature responses.

Elementary children have a large vocabulary, which can easily mask a lack of understanding. Be sure that your students comprehend your meaning. During this period students' reading and writing skills improve greatly and can be used regularly in class work. Be sure to choose material of the appropriate reading level, and do not demand of the children more than they are capable of doing.

Appropriate content for the elementary years includes these concepts: all the world belongs to God; God's love for people who are different in this and other lands; the church as people who love, worship, serve, and share the good news about Jesus; Baptism and Holy Communion (in limited ways); the Bible as a book about God and his ways and his Son Jesus; forgiveness (from age ten, in terms of restored relationships); the days and earthly life of Jesus; heroes of the faith; adventure stories of God's people in the Old and New Testaments; adventure stories of God's people today.

In the elementary years children learn to control and cover up emotions. Society could not survive if we all expressed emotions in the total, impulsive manner of preschoolers. However, parish educators can help the elementary child in two ways: in viewing emotions as a wonderful part of ourselves for which we can thank God, and in helping children learn ways to express emotions in socially acceptable, healthy, and constructive ways rather than "bottling them up."

Socially, elementary children can appreciate others' points of view, but they need help in practicing this skill. Service projects are an excellent opportunity to explain clearly why particular actions will bring joy to certain people.

The family is still the central social influence on the child, although peers become increasingly important, especially toward the end of the period. Children can now recognize family experiences of conditional love and forgiveness that point toward God's unconditional love and forgiveness. Families also provide opportunities for responding to God in loving service. Unfortunately, some of your students may have mainly negative experiences in the family. While it is not possible to overcome such experiences, it is possible to develop a teacher-student relationship of love, care, and forgiveness that will help the child accept a loving and forgiving God.

Students can explore ways in which the gospel may be shared and lived out in the playground, at school, with friends, and with persons who differ from them in appearance, customs, and abilities. Developing positive relationships with persons of all ages is aided by congregational social events such as picnics, potluck suppers, and advent-wreath workshops.

Children need to develop a healthy self-concept. The teacher who is grounded in the gospel will refrain from implying that the child's worth lies in his or her abilities, appearance, or accomplishments. To imply such is to encourage works righteousness, trying to prove one's worth in God's sight by what one is or can do. The gospel tells us that in spite of who we are and what we do, God accepts us out of pure love. With children, emphasize God's undeserved love, which we can always trust no matter how good or bad we feel about ourselves. A self-concept rooted in Baptism understands the self primarily as loved and cherished as God's own child.

Children worship as a result of focusing on God's actions and goodness. Until grade five or six they do not worship "out of the blue" as adults do, because they have so little experience or conceptual framework to draw on. Response to God comes most appropriately during or at the end of a lesson, not at the beginning. Most children thus experience the church service in different ways from adults. Readers enjoy sharing in the congregational responses and hymns, even though many concepts are beyond them. Aspects of the service that appeal to children and can consciously be developed by the parish are music, noise, crowds, color, dramatic movement, pageantry, processions, and even smells. Experiencing the awe and wonder of God in a reverent worship service with all the dignity and ritual of tradition can be a wonderful thing to a child—far better than singling out children for a few minutes of talk in the middle that bears little relation to the rest of the service.

Prayers of elementary children might most helpfully focus on praise and thanksgiving. In the early grades children have a magical view of God's answers to prayer and cannot understand why only some requests are granted. In later grades prayers for self and others become more realistic, and prayer becomes a valued personal conversation with God.

Adolescents

Adolescence is the period between childhood and adulthood, technically beginning at puberty. In our society it is a prolonged period and, by its very length, creates some frustrations for young people.

Physically, adolescence is preceded by a growth spurt, which often results in clumsiness that will tax your imagination in drawing attention away from the unfortunate individual so that he or she will not be the butt of peer jokes. During early adolescence the nervous system and reproductive organs reach maturity. The young person can be helped to appreciate the body as a gift of God that calls for responsible stewardship. While many young teens have access to information about the physical aspects of sexuality, values in the light of the gospel must be an important part of the church's education.

Teenagers come to terms with the permanence of their physical appearance. Joanne realizes that she will not have the face of a movie star after all; Tom faces the fact that he will never develop the physique he had hoped for. The message that God's love does not depend on our looks, abilities, works, or our value in the eyes of our peers can be very good news to teenagers.

In early adolescence, girls are about two years ahead of boys in physical maturity. It is helpful to provide a mixture of activities for a combined boys' and girls' class so that quieter activities alternate with more demanding ones. In grades five to seven, girls grow rapidly and tire easily, while boys are still full of energy. In grades seven to nine the reverse is true.

In the initial stages of abstract thinking, from ages 12 to 14, present doctrine simply and offer few alternative viewpoints, because young teens cannot cope with mental complexity. In middle adolescence, from 15 to 18, students are ready to review theological issues and compare and contrast different points of view. Help youth to see the richness of diversity rather than to harbor prejudice against those who differ. Be sure that students relate their beliefs to practical applications in daily living. Later teens are ready for further complexity and enjoy relating the faith to societal issues. Some go through a period of questioning beliefs as they seek to develop a personal theology; they need support in their quest. Others feel threatened by approaching adulthood and cling to traditional beliefs of their group; they, too, need support and an understanding adult who becomes mentor for them as they face adulthood.

Mentally impaired and gifted adolescents need special attention. Few tasks are as rewarding as preparing for confirmation those who are impaired. By individualizing instruction in the classroom, you can give extra attention to those who need it, or even use differing materials when necessary. Give attention, too, to the gifted—a group often neglected in church education. Capable of serious theological and biblical study, they need to be challenged to deal with issues in depth.

The new ability to introspect results in critical assessment of self, family, and all who are in some sense an extension of the self. Such criticism inevitably results in conflict. The adolescent's critical ability may also be leveled at you. Don't take it personally, and remind yourself that the critical ability is a sign of maturing cognitive development. As the individual turns the critical eye on the self, the gospel brings good news of God's love and forgiveness, as well as the realistic assessment that the person is both simultaneously saved and sinful. In God's analysis, mercy triumphs over judgment.

Early adolescents often delight in traditional worship patterns, which for them are "new" because they now grasp the meaning in a mature way. Middle adolescents may begin to question tradition and prefer some experimentation in worship.

Adolescence can be a moody stage, partly due to hormonal changes and partly to the social situation in which adolescents find themselves. *The* social factor is the desire for independence—a very important achievement that changes the person from someone who is dependent on others to an adult on whom others can depend. Independence is essential to the achievement of constructive adulthood and to mature interdependent relations with another.

In endeavoring to achieve independent adulthood, the individual is confronted with a series of conflicting signals from family and society over a number of years. By 11 or 12, the adolescent begins paying adult fares on transportation; not until 21 is he or she given complete adult status in some areas of responsibility. Two conflicting messages seem constantly leveled at the adolescent: you are a child; you are an adult. This is especially frustrating when signals differ from state to state and from one decade to the next.

In the break from family ties there is inevitable ambiguity. The young person wants independence and yet also the security of childhood and the retention of parental love. Parents want independence for the child and yet are reluctant to relinquish the parental role. Frank discussion with adolescents on relationships with parents in the light of the gospel are helpful, as are classes and independent reading for the parents of adolescents. The Christian educator can also help the adolescent distinguish between social independence and healthy dependence on God.

It used to be thought that identity was a major factor in adolescence—and indeed it is, insofar as the person is developing independence and a sense of independence. But identity, or self-concept, shows remarkable stability during adolescence, developing in a gradual, continuous manner.[12]

In the search for independence, the peer group plays an important role. It assumes some of the authority of the parents and provides a stable support group as the young person breaks away from dependence on the family. In the peer group the adolescent learns how to interact with others, deal with conflict, follow and lead, compromise, and solve problems. Allow time in the learning situation for the development of peer relations. Camps and retreats are excellent settings that provide educational opportunities and time to develop peer relations away from the family setting.

The peer group sets the tone for certain behaviors without which individuals may be unacceptable to the group. Young teens need to learn to resist peer pressure when that is appropriate, and to believe in God's love for unpopular peers.

At first, friendships in adolescence are with members of the same sex. Gradually, dating usually takes over, although same-sex friends continue to act as confidants. Relevant topics in adolescent programs include dating, communications skills, preengagement education, and premarriage and preparenting education.

The adolescent learns adult ways of behaving and values from trusted adults other than family members. Teaching adolescents can be time-consuming, because youth will seek you outside of class time to discuss personal issues. You become a role model for youth in behavior and faith—quite a responsibility! Fortunately, the believing community can support you in prayer and in offering many role models of adulthood for the young persons you teach. In addition, congregations can send caring signals to youth in many ways—by talking to them, providing a special place for them to meet, involving them with mentors in congregational committees, listening to their views, and rejoicing in their idealism that can bring a breath of life to any parish.

The teenage years are a time of important and often life-influencing decisions in vocation, education, and sometimes friends and spouse. The young person makes plans for the future and can understand long-term commitment. Commitment to Christ and the church are deeply personal and long-term; pastors and teachers should be prepared to discuss and rejoice with youth in such commitment. This does not mean that the person "becomes a Christian" at this point; one is a Christian from the time of one's Baptism. But the adolescent is able to affirm personally his or her intention to remain true to that Baptism.

Confirmation is part of a lifelong pastoral and educational ministry through which God strengthens the baptized by Word and sacrament and prepares them to share in the church's mission. Many adolescents seek some outward manifestation of that process in a rite—whether in one or more Affirmation of Baptism services or in a certificate indicating that they have completed a particular period of study. Probably the church needs to send signals more often and clearly to adolescents that they are recognized as mature, responsible persons. Some parishes designate particular areas of service that teens recognize as a sign of their maturity (such as ushering or being admitted to the senior music program). If the parish has no such signals, the youth will make their own. Unfortunately, one such common signal is found in parishes with little adult education. Youth reason that the adult pattern is to cease studying, so they rejoice when they "graduate" from learning. Such a situation is tragic.

Adults

Adulthood is not a unified experience, but a vast variety of experiences and growth. Some writers speak of stages.[13] Unfortunately, in parish education we often act as if all adults were a homogeneous conglomerate. We speak of "the adult class" or "the Lenten Bible study for the parish adults," as if all adults could or should be involved in the same program. Perhaps one of the greatest changes in educational planning that we need is to take serious account of variety in programming for adults.

First, we should say something of the ways in which adults typically learn, whatever stage they are in. You might ask yourself which of these characteristics is true of you when you are in a volunteer learning situation (as opposed, say, to taking courses to prepare for a career).

Adult learners are often insecure. They have a reputation to maintain and fear making mistakes. Question-and-answer techniques work well only with very secure adults. Discussion is enhanced by a high level of trust in the group.

Adults are oriented to solving life's problems. They are practical and want to know how a course or book will be useful in the near future.

Adults have many experiences which should be welcomed by leaders as useful resources in learning. Sometimes you may need to guide participants so that experiences are shared briefly and in relevant ways. The adult learner expects to be respected by the group leader and participants. Group members may expect to participate in planning topics, programs, or time and place of meeting. The more you encourage self-directed behavior, the more you will help participants feel that they are valued and respected members. Contemporary writers on adult religious education sometimes use Knowles' concept of andragogy, an approach that takes seriously the adults' experience, independence, and self-directed behavior in learning.[14]

Adults may participate in educational programs for many reasons. Some participate in order to prepare for a task (such as developing a stewardship program or serving on the worship committee) or to deal with an issue they face at work or home (such as making ethical decisions in business or parenting adolescents). Some participate for pure love of learning about the faith. And some attend groups mainly for social reasons, resisting suggestions that they prepare for class or engage in learning in depth. Some may even come out of guilt or because it has always been done. There are parents who come to be an example to their children. It is always wise to check the reasons why your participants are involved so that you can judge the appropriateness of methods and depth of content. Often adults have mixed motives in attending.

In group settings adults often appreciate a comfortable environment, time to chat over coffee before or after, and "prestige" (some sign that the course is important, such as the cost of a textbook). Many adults prefer short-term commitments of five to seven weeks. Busy personal or family schedules may result in sporadic attendance, in which case topics that can be completed in a single session are appropriate.

Many adults today have busy schedules that preclude attendance at groups and classes. They prefer the freedom to learn in their own time. Essential in the parish is a good up-to-date library of books, tapes, religious magazines, and perhaps videotapes, with a clearly organized borrowing system. Also helpful are persons with whom to discuss reading or a parish "educational hotline" operating at certain hours to deal with questions.

Following are brief comments on the phases of adulthood and their implications for Christian education.

Young adulthood

Young adults are developing intimate relations with others. They are interested in communications skills, solving conflict, forgiving, expressing intimacy, and how the gospel relates to these issues. Other concerns include leaving the parental nest or family of origin, training for vocation, preparing for possible marriage, exploring the possibility of parenting, and dealing with being single—either as a transitional or permanent state. Young adults often move from one vocation to another or from one study program to another; they seek an understanding of the doctrine of vocation as well as ethical values.

As the idealism of later adolescence becomes tempered with realism, young adults seek a vision of society and the church with which they can operate comfortably. In the peak of physical capabilities and athletic achievement, young adults are also interested in health issues and stewardship of physical resources. In taking responsibility for finances, they seek guidance in the light of the gospel.

Young adults enjoy learning from one another's experiences. It is helpful to give opportunity for social interaction in which such informal learning can take place. The teacher of young adults may expect to spend more time than the teacher of middle adults, because many young adults look to a trusted person as mentor as they move to full inner dependence.

Since young adults are often busy with work, study, establishing a permanent relationship with another, and sometimes parenting, the religious educator has to provide a variety of learning opportunities, including independent study, which can be fitted into odd time slots at the individual's convenience.

From young adult to midlife

From 25 to 40 years the person moves from early adulthood to midlife. At present, the baby boom following World War II has increased the numbers in this category. In the decades ahead parish education should take account of the increase successively through to older adulthood as the baby boom ages.

Adults can reflect in mature ways on theological, biblical, and ethical issues and should be encouraged to relate their learning to their everyday ministry in the world as well as in the church. We can capitalize on the fact that these are the peak years for intellectual achievement. Relevant topics include the ministry of the whole people of God, a deeper look at Christian vocation, the priesthood of all believers, the opportunity to evaluate the mission of the church and the individual's role in it, stewardship of increasing possessions, issues for singles, marriage enrichment, and parenting skills—especially the parenting of adolescents.

Toward the end of the 30s, as midlife approaches, many persons reevaluate career choices, married or single life-styles, and ideals. They realize that now may be their last chance to have a child, change a career, or retool for another career. They also realize that early dreams and expectations may never be fulfilled, which calls for an adjustment to reality. Grief education is helpful in dealing with lost hopes and ideals, broken marriages, and career changes.

Some learners may want to deal with conflicting financial responsibilities, such as paying tuition for offspring while helping aging parents; the grief of losing the dependence of young children and the prospect of the "empty nest" ahead; aging and death of parents, and therefore the prospect of their own aging and eventual death.

The years prior to midlife are busy ones with little spare time, as adults acquire possessions, raise families, and become more involved in relationships at work, home, and in society. This period may not be the best for groups and classes, especially for persons with hectic and unpredictable schedules, who find independent learning more appropriate.

In planning, bear in mind that this age bracket is often likely to be conservative, because it is responsible for an up-and-coming generation, and so is less likely to experiment with radical ideas and programs.

From midlife to retirement

From 40 to 65 years, as persons move from midlife to retirement, they may have more time to devote to learning. Groups and classes therefore may be more appropriate. Family responsibilities are lessened, and the career ladder has probably been climbed sufficiently for the person to relax a little.

Many persons have social authority or achievement and are interested in relating their faith to their responsibilities. By the mid 50s, adults have more personalized enjoyments and more freedom to be independent and self-sufficient. Many show more tolerance and satisfaction, a mellowing that allows experimentation with ideas and programs that earlier they would have questioned.

Issues they may want to address include adjusting to singleness, remarriage, or a new career (as a result of midlife change); death and grief, especially if parents or friends have died; communicating with spouse and adult friends, skills often lost over the years and now in need of sharpening as children leave home; preretirement education and stewardship of time; vocation in retirement; grandparenting skills; helping children or grandchildren pray and learn of God; relating to one's adult children; and dealing with the gradual decline in physical functioning.

Older adults

Adults 65 years and older will be growing in numbers in our society in coming decades. Nor can parish educators treat older persons as a homogeneous bunch—there are the young old, the old, and the old old, at the very least.[15]

One of the richest resources in parish education with older adults is the learners' long experience of life and faith, which should be integrated into the learning process.

Topical areas that concern many older adults include adjustment to retirement and finding avenues of service, health and financial issues, deciding where to live, preparing for or adjusting to death of spouses and close friends, learning to live alone, understanding the aging process and preparing for death, and becoming dependent gracefully.

At present, older adults probably have more time than other phases of adulthood. Because women tend to outlive men, many older adults are single women. Groups and classes can be held effectively in conjunction with social activities. Trips are an excellent opportunity to combine learning and fun. If many persons live alone in the neighborhood and may be tempted to skimp on cooking for themselves, a meal following the learning experience can be a worthwhile social, as well as nutritional, addition.

Weekly programs for older persons should allow for sporadic attendance due to health problems, need to care for a sick spouse or friend, and difficulty in driving in inclement weather. Many older persons appreciate daytime groups so they do not have to drive at night. Education on church premises is possible only if the elderly can easily and safely enter the buildings and work comfortably with the materials. Handrails, ramps, large-print resources, and so on, should be considered.

When older persons become homebound for shorter or longer periods, parishes can offer independent learning opportunities or one-to-one opportunities through visitation programs. Visitors may want to take a prepared tape, an excerpt from a book to read aloud, or a list of questions to spark thought as the two watch a tape on the VCR or view a television program. Active older adults might help prepare such items for the homebound

Parishes must also take responsibility for education in the institutional settings in their neighborhoods. While only a small percentage of older adults are institutionalized, they may easily be the forgotten minority. They are still capable of learning if time and opportunity are given.

EIGHT

CHRISTIAN EDUCATION: AN EXERCISE IN INTERPRETING

A. Roger Gobbel

Christian education, as discussed in this chapter, is the work of engaging Christians in an ongoing hermeneutical or interpretive task. As such, it necessarily includes instruction in the contents of the faith, but moves beyond that boundary. It strives to assist and to challenge Christians to interpret their lives and the world with its things, events, and people under the life, death, and resurrection of Jesus. It encourages them in the task of making sense of and achieving meaning for themselves as the people of God, and living faithfully in those meanings. The work of interpretation is an ongoing, lifelong task in which children, adolescents, and adults participate.

Over the past decade, an increasing number of persons, with varying emphases and concerns, have explored Christian education as an engagement in interpretation. Edward Everding, a New Testament scholar with a concern for educational theory in the church, asserted that "hermeneutics provides the proper frame of reference in which to develop" theory for Christian education.[1] For him, a hermeneutical approach to Christian education, while giving significant attention to content, will at the same time give emphasis to the nature of interpretation and understanding. Berard Marthaler, espousing a theory of Christian education as a process of socialization, concluded, "Catechesis begins

139

as an exercise in hermeneutics. Education becomes a lesson in interpreting one's personal experiences as well as historical events in the light of the faith."[2] Jack Seymour and Carol Wehrheim, asserting that Christian education is to bring the faith story and the experience of living into a dialogical relationship, added, "Christian education seeks to help persons make meaning of the Christ of God and live faithfully in terms of that meaning."[3] Both Thomas Groome's description of Christian education as a "present dialectical hermeneutics"[4] and that of Douglas Wingeier as "faith translation"[5] are essentially models of an interpretive task. Both give attention to the content of the faith to be interpreted, to the life content of the interpreter which also must be interpreted, and to the interaction between content to be interpreted and the interpreter. John Peatling, vigorously and persistently calling for the utilization of the construct of human development in the work of Christian education, asserted that every interpretation involves a human interpreter who is a "thoroughly developmental creature" and "who is at some place, level or 'stage' in a developmental sequence."[6]

To approach Christian education as an exercise in interpreting can assist us to reconsider and examine many of our already held presuppositions. It can challenge us to reshape our theory of Christian education and our doing of the enterprise.

Interpreting: A Continuing Activity

Everding asserted that "all of life is an interpretation"[7] and that, quoting Richard Palmer, the activity of interpreting is "perhaps the most basic act of human thinking; indeed, existing itself may be said to be a constant process of interpretation."[8] Here we will describe the activity of interpreting as the process by which individuals make sense of, achieve meanings for, or create and construct understandings of self, the world, and human life. The sense made, meanings achieved, or understandings constructed give coherence and direction to one's own life, and inform and shape values, commitments, and behaviors.

In the description we will utilize the perspective of developmental constructivism emerging from the study of human development.[9] In broad terms, that perspective holds that "individuals, acting upon and interacting with the world outside them and with their experiences in it, are in the process of constructing and learning to construct their own understandings or meanings."[10] In Chapter 7, Margaret Krych discussed the multiple dimensions of human development, including the construct of developmental sequences. Her discussion amplifies Peatling's assertion that we are "thoroughly developmental creatures" who are "at some place, level or 'stage' in a development sequence." How one participates in the activity of interpreting and the results of that activity will always be determined by developmental abilities and limitations, determined by the place that one stands at the moment in the developmental sequence.

Constructing understanding

We are born with no innate knowledge or understanding of self, the world, and human life. From birth to death, all persons are engaged in the essential, ongoing, and complex human task of making sense, achieving meaning, or constructing understandings. The process begins in infancy. We are all dependent on our external world to provide us information and experiences about which we can think and feel, information and experiences on which we can act and with which we can interact. As we think, feel, act on, and interact with the information and experience, we achieve our own meanings for them and create our own understandings of them.

Throughout life we are confronted by an enormous array of information, stimuli, and experiences from the external world. Clearly, we cannot attend to all that is offered. As we think, feel, act on, and interact with, we by necessity turn our attention to but a portion of what is offered. Deliberately or unintentionally, consciously or unconsciously, we determine the information and experiences about which we will think and feel. As we act on and interact on those things, we give order to them, make sense of them, and construct our own understandings of them. We create an internal picture of the world, self, and human life, and that picture functions as reality for us.

Whatever the picture created, the meanings achieved, or the understandings constructed, the individual is using but a portion of the information and experiences available. Moreover, not all individuals select the same set of information and experiences to which attention is given. Also, recognizing that different individuals have differing development abilities and limitations and have differing experiences with which to think and feel, we can expect a rich and wide diversity of understandings, meanings, or sense made. The point is simple. No two persons understand the world and human life in exactly the same way, and we should not expect anything different.

As we act on and interact with information and experiences within the construct of developmental sequences, we achieve our meanings or understandings. Those understandings or meanings are both necessary and critical, and to them we will be committed. We will hold them as valuable and as truth. Our achieved understandings will influence profoundly how we will act on and respond to the world, to others, and to our experiences. They will serve to influence and shape new understandings, because we view the world through understandings already achieved. At the same time, our already achieved understandings or meanings will influence how we will permit the world and events to impinge on us. They will influence our decisions concerning those things that merit our attention and consideration.

A critical element of the perspective of developmental constructivism calls for emphasis here. The individual is an active participant in the work of interpreting, achieving meaning, or constructing understanding. The individual is an active participant in making sense of the world, giving to it or its parts value and worth. Meaning or understanding is not some "thing" that can be transmitted from one person to another in a one-to-one correspondence. The individual must construct his or her own understanding. A person cannot do that task for another. Thus far, emphasis has been given to the essential role of the individual in the interpretive process, but the process is not merely a privatistic matter. Significant and necessary communal dimensions are also active. To these we will turn presently.

A continuing activity

The infant participates in the activity of interpreting. The infant must make some sense of the world for himself or herself. The primary caretaker provides the infant with an array of experiences and stimuli with which he or she can act and interact. In the acting and interacting the infant constructs some "picture" of self, the world, and others. Encumbered by cognitive, affective, and social limitations, the young child's making sense may be most simplistic and undifferentiated. Most basic, however, is the assertion that regardless of how that "picture" may be described, it is of the child's own making and belongs to the child. At the same time it is clear that the child is dependent on others—a community—for information and experiences.

Over the life span the individual is an active participant in elaborating on already achieved meanings or understandings. That is, the individual has the possibility of altering, rearranging, expanding on, and even transforming already achieved understandings. There is the possibility that the individual can achieve new or at least somewhat different interpretations or understandings that are more complex, differentiated, and inclusive.

Three factors may challenge the individual to engage in the elaboration process, in the continuing activity of interpreting.

First, in the presence of new circumstances, information, and experiences, already achieved understandings may prove to be insufficient to deal with and respond to the new. If the individual is to respond to the challenges of the new, then alterations, rearrangement, or even transformations may be necessary. Interacting with the world, its events, things, and people, the individual encounters challenges and conflicts that both call into question already achieved interpretations and call forth new understandings.

Second, over the life span the individual has an increasing range of experience. The individual has a more complex and differentiated life content with which to explore the world and life in it. That increasing range of experience enables and calls the individual to see, to understand the world in new ways.

Third, with the increased cognitive, affective, and social abilities, the individual is enabled to see the world in new dimensions, enabled to ask new questions of the world with its things, events, and people, and enabled to construct and achieve new understandings. In new seasons and circumstances, with an increasing range of experience and with increased developmental abilities, the individual may remember and recall, muse and think about past events, personal experiences, information received in the past, and present understandings. Recalling, thinking, and feeling about, acting on and interacting with the past, the individual may reinterpret the past and come to understand it in different and new ways. In a sense, a new world is entered.

Several implications in the discussion thus far must be highlighted.

First, the continuing activity of interpreting is in continuity with the past. The past influences our interpretive activity in the present. Understandings achieved in the past and past experiences impinge on the present. At the same time, the interpretive activity can assist us to come to new understandings of the past, even as the past serves to inform and shape our present.

Second, though we may regard our present understandings in some absolute fashion and though we may be profoundly committed to them, we yet need to regard them with some degree of tentativeness. New experiences are yet to be known, and new information to be gained. In the presence of the new we will engage in continuing interpretation, in the process of altering, rearranging, and even transforming.

Third, we would do well to refrain from making quick judgments of "right" and "wrong" with reference to another's achieved understanding. We may wish to challenge, to ask for clarification, and ask questions of another's understanding. But above all, it is essential to remember that another's achieved understanding belongs to that person. It is the result of that person's attempt to understand the world. It may represent the best that the individual may achieve at the moment within the context of his or her developmental abilities and limitations, the information possessed, and range of experience. This is not to suggest that we benignly tolerate "just anything." Rather, it is to recognize the difference between persons as they participate in the interpretive process and to respect those differences. It is to appreciate the task that each individual must do for himself or herself.

Interpreting in community

The activity of interpreting, while an individual task, is not a privatistic task. The individual is always dependent on the outside world, various communities, and other persons to provide information, events, and experiences about which one can think and feel and on which we

act and interact. We are members of a culture, a society, and particular
communities that offer particular information, events, and experience.
Thus there will always be communal dimensions to the hermeneutical
task.

Cultures, societies, and communities are themselves expressions of
achieved understandings. They are human constructions. A particular
community lives in the world as an expression of ordering, interpreting,
thinking, and feeling about that world. It has its rituals and documents
that serve both to describe its members and to maintain its existence.
By its life it sets forth ways of behaving toward, acting on, and interacting with the world or some segment of it. In some dimensions a
community will define limits and ways of thinking, feeling, and valuing
that are deemed acceptable and that are expected of its people. Pre-
scribed behaviors, the community's values and norms, and its expectations are means by which the community strives to shape the interpretation and understanding of its members. These are the information
and experiences that a community offers to its people. The very language of the community calls its members to give attention to specific
information and events and provides members with a means to describe
the world in particular ways.

A particular community can be expected to initiate, maintain, and
challenge its members in its particular way of thinking, feeling, believing, and evaluating. Deliberately and intentionally, it will call its
people to think and feel about specific events, experiences, and expectations. It will provide its members with specific information and
experiences that it holds valuable, while consciously excluding others.
It will deliberately do those things to assist, encourage, and challenge
its members to claim for themselves its way of interpreting and understanding. Thus the community works to assist its members to
achieve commonly held and shared understandings.

Even as the community does its necessary work of socialization, the
community should not summarily impose its understandings on its
members. Whatever things the community may do, whatever experiences and information it may provide, individuals encounter them, act
on them, and interact with them within the context of abilities and
limitations, within their range of experience, and within the context of

their already achieved understandings. In the end, individuals must interpret and construct for themselves their own understandings of the community, its contents, its offered experiences, its ways of doing things, and their place in the community. Through engagement and conversations with the community's contents and with each other, the community's people may achieve a high degree of commonality in interpreting, understanding, valuing, and behaving. At the same time, the engagement and conversations may serve to alter, rearrange, and even transform the contents and even the life of the community. Yet even though sharing in the life of the community, each individual is responsible for his or her participation in the interpreting activity and for the understandings he or she constructs. The community must work to assist and encourage its people to engage in an essential human task, to participate in the activity of interpreting as richly and profoundly as they are able.[11] Thus there is always a continuing dialectic between the individual and the community, a dialectic characterized by conversation, challenge, conflict, and questions as individuals live in community.

Two Theological Considerations

The perspective of developmental constructivism, emerging from the study of human development, is one description of the essential and continuing human activity of interpreting and constructing understanding. It is necessary and proper to ask if this perspective can serve any useful purpose in the work of Christian education. In what ways might this perspective inform the theory and practice of Christian education?

The human creatures

Some may assert that we must not permit the field of human development with its perspective of constructivism to determine any part of the agenda of Christian education. To receive and joyfully use findings from that field in the service of Christian education is regarded by some as a retreat from—even as abandonment of—theology and the Bible. Certainly, findings from the field are not to be embraced uncritically or used indiscriminately. They are to be scrutinized carefully and challenged when necessary. But at the same time, theology and the Bible do not and cannot afford descriptions of human development. They are not equipped for such a work. It is essential that we move outside theology and the Bible for significant data related to human development.

Findings from the field may challenge much that we normally do in Christian education. They may challenge some of the things that we want to believe about the human creature. Nevertheless, we must take with utmost seriousness a major theological consideration. If those in the field of human development are, in any sense, appropriately describing the human creature, appropriately describing the cognitive, affective, and social development, appropriately describing development sequences across the life span, and appropriately describing the essential human task of interpreting, making sense, and constructing understanding—then they are appropriately describing God's creation, human beings loved and cherished by God. If we choose to ignore or to dismiss lightly those appropriate findings, we may well refuse to take seriously God's creation.

Those working in the field of human development may or may not make such claims concerning God's creation. In their efforts to achieve some understanding of human development, they are not necessarily making statements about God, the Bible, Jesus, faith, or salvation. They are not necessarily concerned with any Christian categories. What may or may not be the theological posture of those in the field is not a concern here, but if they are appropriately describing human development, they are describing God's creatures whom we are to love, cherish, and respect.

At the same time, Christian tradition takes seriously other realities of the human creature. For example, it always recognizes the broken condition of human beings, as individuals or communities. It takes seriously the destructiveness of sin and the havoc that sin produces in human life, both to persons and communities. Christians are both "saints and sinners." As Christians seek to come to terms with the world and life in it and strive to achieve understanding, sin remains. Thus we ought not to expect of the interpretive process what is unrealistic. The results of the process may be for "good" or for "bad."

Most normally, we can expect a disturbing, even distressing, mixture of the two. And so we are constantly challenged to engage the process anew.

Baptism

Baptism holds a central place in Lutheran tradition. It informs, defines, and shapes Christian education in significant and critical dimensions. In the Sacrament of Baptism, claims are made and promises announced. We are liberated from the power of sin and death, and we are joined to the death and resurrection of our Lord Jesus Christ. Born children of a "fallen humanity," "we are reborn children of God and inheritors of eternal life." We are sealed by the Holy Spirit and "marked by the cross of Christ forever." We are brought into the Lord's family and made members of the body of Christ.[12]

The claims and promises are God's claims and promises. They are declared to infants as well as to adults. Whether we consider the Baptism of an infant or an adult, completeness and wholeness are marks of those claims and promises. Some things are settled with finality, completeness, and wholeness. To whom we belong and who we are are matters that have been determined. We belong to God, are claimed by God, and are children of God, inheritors of eternal life. Nothing need be or can be added to our Baptism. Nothing is yet to be done to complete our Baptism. God's work is complete.

Between our Baptism and death, we are to live the baptismal life in faith. In the world, we are to be, to live, and to do who we already are—children of God. While Baptism is complete and whole, life in Baptism is always marked by surprises, the unexpected, and an amazing and exciting newness. Time and time again, we ask the question, What does it mean for me to be a baptized person? Responses to this question will result from active participation in the process of interpretation and the work of constructing understandings of ourselves as baptized persons.

The responses we give to the question, while proper, right, and faithful for today, may not be proper, right, and faithful for tomorrow. We may be committed to our responses and regard them in some sense as absolute, but we dare not regard them as final, complete, or un-changeable. In new seasons and situations we encounter new events and new demands, calling us to remember anew who we are, requiring us to ask the question again, and challenging us to achieve new un-derstandings and responses never imagined or anticipated. We have the task of making new sense and constructing new understandings of ourselves as the people of God. Life in Baptism is always a life of interpreting. Thus, our understandings and the content of our life in Baptism will vary, alter, and even change radically across the life span.

How we come to understand baptismal life and how we live out that life will always be determined in part by the fact that we are at some point, some place in a developmental sequence. As they participate in the life of a Christian community, children participate in the interpretive process. They are not the passive recipients of ready-made answers. Within the context of their abilities and limitations, range of experience, and circumstances, they do achieve or construct their understandings of themselves in relationship to the world, God, Jesus, and the church. Not utilizing the language of adults and not having the content of those belonging to adults, those understandings are always characteristic of children and belong to children. Because they possess new and larger abilities and enjoy a wider range of experience, adolescents can achieve new and more complex understandings of themselves as God's people. Adults continue to interpret and respond anew to the question, What does it mean for me this day to be a baptized person?

Christian education is always the work of calling Christians to re-member who they are and challenging them to live life in Baptism. It is the work of assisting them to make sense of themselves as God's people and to assist them to live baptismal life as they are able within the context of their abilities and limitations and within their times and circumstances. Christian education is for all ages. As Christians share in this exercise or activity of interpreting, there is always the expec-tation and anticipation of knowing that new understandings of and responses to God, Jesus, the church, and themselves as a baptized people are yet to be achieved.

Interpretation and Content

Interpretation requires a content to be interpreted. In the Christian church, we have our liturgies, cultic acts, particular stories, sacred texts, and confessional writings. These constitute, in part, the content of Christian education. These contents we cherish, hold to be valuable, and regard in some sense as truth. They identify and describe us as a particular people. They serve to nurture us in the faith. They serve to shape our lives as Christian people. These contents must have a prominent role in Christian education.

In many respects, the contents of the faith are constant. The contents of the faith are themselves the results of the interpretive activity, the results of faithful men and women striving to make sense of, to achieve some understandings of what God had done, was doing, and was yet to do. For example, the Bible, remaining constant in its own content, does not tell one single, unified story. Rather, it tells many and diverse stories, even different stories of the same thing. In the Bible we encounter faithful men and women, bearing witness in their times and circumstances to what God had done, was doing, and was yet to do. They engaged in the activity of interpreting. And time and time again, we encounter new, amazing, and unexpected stories. Moreover, the very development of the canon itself resulted from the activity of interpreting.

Through the centuries, in new seasons and circumstances and in the presence of new problems and demands, the church has engaged anew in the interpretive process, asking, What is it this day to be the body of Christ? The understandings and responses that the church has given across the centuries have not been uniform and singular. Various confessional writings are themselves the results of interpretation. The church itself has interpreted and reinterpreted its sacred texts and contents as it has sought to understand itself as the body of Christ and to respond faithfully. To speak of Christian education as an exercise in engaging Christians in the activity is nothing more or less than to engage them in proper and necessary tasks characteristic of the church through the ages.

A faith tradition interprets what God has done

Every particular Christian faith tradition is a mode of interpreting all life and the world under the life, death, and resurrection of Jesus Christ. Every Christian faith tradition stands in the world as an interpretation of what God has done, is doing, and is yet to do. It stands as a way of thinking and feeling about Jesus. It lives as a way of behaving and responding as a people of God. A Christian faith tradition is not static. It, too, has participated in the continuing activity of interpreting. The stories that it tells of itself today are often quite different from the stories it told of itself yesterday. New interpretations of what it is to be a particular people of God have been achieved. Yet, engaging in interpretation and creating new stories, it remains in continuity with its past, while yet achieving new understandings and responses not expected, not anticipated, and not even possible yesterday. Through the activity of interpreting tradition has been added to tradition. Christian education is to assist Christians in community to engage in the same work.

Every particular faith tradition is a way of thinking and feeling about and making sense of the life, death, and resurrection of Jesus. Each has its cultic acts, stories, sacred texts, and confessional writings. It is right and proper that a tradition will strive to initiate and maintain its members and its ways of thinking, feeling, behaving, and valuing. It is right and proper that the tradition bring its particular, even unique, contents to bear on its people. They give expression to what the tradition profoundly believes, holds valuable, and cherishes. They give shape to the life of a people. The faith community will challenge its members to share and participate in its ways of thinking, believing, valuing, and behaving.

As a tradition returns to its contents for guidance and instruction, it asks not only, What might those things have meant to the faithful in the past? but also, What might they mean for us today? Between the two sets of responses there may be amazing, even radical, differences. Yet both can be judged faithful in their own times.

The shape of Christian education

Briefly, what might be the shape of Christian education as an exercise in interpreting?

First, the contents of the tradition—its sacred texts, cultic acts, stories, and confessional writings—are to be presented forcefully and clearly. Its way of thinking, feeling, believing, and behaving are to be declared.

Second, Christian education is an invitation to engage, examine, and explore the contents of the tradition. Engaging them, Christians together ask not only, What might these things have meant to the faithful in the past? but, What might these things mean for us today? Each must ask these questions within the context of his or her abilities and life content. New visions and understandings of what God has done, is doing, and is yet to do are always present possibilities.

Third, Christian education is characterized by acts of witnessing. Christians will give witness to the faith of the church and their own faith in that church. Thus Christian education is a conversation together in the faith.

Fourth, in the conversation Christians will encourage and support each other. At the same time, there will be challenge and questioning. Sharp and probing questions will be asked of each other. And all will be challenged time and time again to reexamine their interpretations and to consider them anew against the backdrop of the life, death, and resurrection of Jesus.

Fifth, Christian education will assist, encourage and challenge Christians, both individually and communally, to respond daily to two questions: What is it for me this day to be a baptized person? and, What is it for us together this day to be the people of God?[13]

Interpreting is a necessary activity of the church

Christian education for Christians in community is to encourage, challenge, and assist boys and girls, women and men, to engage in the continuing activity of interpreting that is so characteristic of the church and its particular traditions.

Moreover, it is a necessary activity of the church and its people as they strive for some understanding of what God has done, is doing, and is yet to do. It is a necessary activity as Christians strive for some understanding of themselves as God's people and as they seek to live baptismal life faithfully. Christians must do that task for themselves within their present contexts of abilities, experiences, circumstances, and demands. Thus we can expect and celebrate a rich and wide diversity that may be achieved.

Christian education is for Christians in community. It is in Christian community that the Holy Spirit is at work enlightening the people of God. And so, as Christians move across the life span, we live in joyful expectation and anticipation that new stories of ourselves as God's people are yet to be told, that we will hear things not yet heard, that we will understand in ways not possible, that our lives will be shaped in ways unimagined now, and that we will see visions not yet dreamed.

NINE

A LUTHERAN APPROACH TO TEACHING

Kent L. Johnson

A teaching/learning experience is a spontaneous event. And while the learning may be significant or relatively inconsequential in such an experience, that may be all that it is—spontaneous. Many teaching/ learning experiences, however, are more than that. For lack of a better word, one could say that they are planned. The more carefully they are planned by the teacher, and the more dimensions that are taken into account in them, the more one could say that such experiences represent an approach to teaching. In this chapter I raise the question: Is there an approach to teaching that could be called "Lutheran"? And, having raised that question, I respond with an essay that I hope will lead to an approach to teaching that is consistent and appropriate for Lutherans. Before looking at a Lutheran approach that exists today, I will briefly review concerns for teaching and learning that influenced education in the Lutheran tradition.

A Brief Historical Sketch

The reformers of the 16th century were vitally concerned for teaching. As Martin Luther prepared for and taught his classes on the Psalms, he began to lay the foundations for the events that would shake the church. During his lifetime he expressed confidence in an educational program, supported by the civil government, that would enable the German people to be good citizens of both state and church. When he discovered the religious illiteracy of both priests and laity in the church of his time, he wrote a catechism that was designed to correct that deficiency. Eventually that catechism would become the primer for almost all who would come to adult membership in the Lutheran church.[1]

As a teacher, Luther surrounded himself with teachers. One was Philip Melancthon, whose interest in education was so great that he was given the title, "The Teacher of Germany."[2] Others, like Johann Bugenhagen and Johann Sturm, were kept busy visiting, evaluating, and establishing schools in Protestant lands. For several centuries educational offerings and opportunities were guided by the codes and values enunciated by these reformers.[3]

With that kind of an orientation, it might seem strange that the Lutheran Confessions say very little about the church's ministry of teaching. In Article 7 of the Augsburg Confession, Melanchthon stated that the church is where the gospel is preached and the sacraments are rightly administered.[4] That phrase, so often quoted as a basis for a ministry of Word and sacrament, seems to ignore, or consign to a place of relative unimportance, the teaching ministry of the church. Such an understanding would not be consistent with Melanchthon's high regard for the teaching office. That regard is evident in the way that he began many of the clauses in that confession: "Our churches teach. . . ."[5]

For Melanchthon, as well as the other reformers, it was implicitly understood that the very identity of the church required it to teach. So basic was this understanding that there was little need to make the point explicitly. Occupying a sure and necessary place in the life of the church, however, afforded no independent existence for teaching in the reformers' overall scheme of things. Teaching was always related to what the church confessed in its preaching and upheld in its participation in the sacraments. Within the content and context of the means of grace by which the Holy Spirit created and sustained faith, teaching enabled the church to be the church. Teachers and teaching were not options in the life of the church that needed to be justified and defended; they were simply understood as necessary.

It may be that just as the reformers took it for granted that there would be teaching in the church, so also they assumed there would be learning. And, if learning was a given, then there was no great need to reflect on *how* learning occurred, or in what ways teaching enhanced it. If not concerned for learning as such, they were interested in curriculum. Everyone in Lutheran lands was to be offered a basic education. Those students who displayed a capacity for more advanced study were to be given exposure to a curriculum dominated by the classical liberal arts.[6] If Luther did not give a great deal of attention to how learning occurred, he *did* recognize that not all people had an equal ability to learn these liberal arts. As accurate as that observation may have been, and as freeing as that may have been for those who couldn't, or wouldn't, submit themselves to those academic disciplines, it left the burden for learning on the learner. And as long as learning remained a subordinate factor in the teaching/learning relationship, the consideration of approaches to teaching also remained a relatively unimportant consideration.

It would be hard to pinpoint where and when learning began to be an important issue for teachers. Before the advent of Jesus Christ, the Greeks reflected on the issue. Among the Romans, teachers such as Quintilian and Plutarch continued the discussion in their writings. Experimental schools that gave serious attention to learning were established in Italy as early as the 13th century.[7] In the beginning years of the 17th century, Johann Comenius wrote books and started schools that reflected his interest in learning.[8] Johann Pestalozzi continued that interest and gave impetus to the notion that those who teach should be prepared to do so.[9] Once that idea had gained some acceptance, the matter of approaches to teaching had to follow. Among the first to make recommendations was Johann F. Herbart. His five-step approach to teaching (preparation, presentation, association, generalization, and application), it was argued, led to increased and sound learning.[10]

Not long into the 20th century, social scientists joined the philosophers in reflecting on human learning. J. B. Watson, E. L. Thorndike, I. P. Pavlov, B. F. Skinner, K. Koffka, K. Lewin, and J. Piaget, among others, brought the tools of science to the task, to assist them in their examination of the question as to how humans learn. Data generated by the research of persons such as these has resulted in many theories as to how teachers should approach their teaching, and to debates as to which is the best.

A Definition of Approaches to Teaching

Approaches to teaching can be described on at least two levels. On one level, an approach is what can be seen and experienced by students and others as they observe how teachers function—the kinds of relationships they establish, where they locate themselves with respect to students as they teach, their use of control and authority, and the methods they use in their teaching. On another level, approaches to teaching refer to the informed and valued judgments teachers make with regard to several questions. These judgments influence, if they don't always determine, how teachers are with their students. Among those questions are these: What is the purpose for teaching/learning? Who is the teacher? Who is the learner? What is the context for teaching/learning? Can learning be evaluated? If so, how?

Using questions such as these, Harold Burgess examined the work of many in the field of religious education. He found that those he analyzed represented four general approaches to teaching (traditional, social-cultural, contemporary-theological, social service).[11] In their book *Contemporary Approaches to Christian Education,* Jack Seymour and others describe five approaches (religious instruction, faith community, spiritual development, liberation, interpretation).[12] Thomas Groome, deftly combining his rich background in biblical and philosophical foundations with current research in the areas of learning and faith development, proposed a shared praxis approach in his book, *Christian Religious Education.*[13] John Peating, in *Religious Education in a Psychological Key,* identified how the insights of several learning theorists could shape approaches to teaching in the church.[14]

With all the possibilities available to us, which approach best meets our needs? And, returning to the question raised in the introduction to this chapter, is there such a thing as a Lutheran approach to teaching? If there is, what are its components? And of those components, which are to be the dominant ones?

Whatever responses can be given to the secondary questions above, I am confident that with respect to the main question, the answer is that there is no single approach to teaching that could be called "Lutheran." Although it isn't always practiced, freedom is so inherent in the Lutheran ethos that once an approach had been offered as *the* way for Lutherans to go, there would be a host to object. Acknowledging that, however, does not mean that there aren't ways that Lutherans can respond to the above questions. There is much in our tradition that can, and does, inform the way we teach. But from what perspective should one begin? There are several possibilities available to us.

One is to go outside the tradition and begin, as did John Peating, with data available to us through the social sciences. Lutherans have been free to use the ideas of Erik Erikson, James Fowler, and Jean Piaget—to mention but a few—in their writing and editing of curriculum materials. Could not one or the other provide, as well, a point of departure in developing "a" Lutheran approach to teaching? I think that would be a good way to proceed. In any case, finally, this material must be taken into account in the formulation of a teaching approach. For my purposes here, however, I did not select that option.

Other possibilities include the Bible or the Lutheran Confessions as points of departure for an approach to teaching.

The basic themes of Lutheran theology could provide yet another reference point for the discussion. Carl Braaten's *Principles of Lutheran Theology* would be an excellent example of such a resource.[15] Once again, however, I chose not to take that route. Rather, I was led by a comment Braaten made to select another.

Braaten argued that worship had played an important role in maintaining a healthy outlook toward Scripture. He then went on to say:

> There is no teaching office in the church that can give a decisive answer to any question of faith and morals which does not ground its teaching in the common norm of all Christianity, and that is conveyed by Scripture alone. In this sense we can and must still maintain the principle of *sola scriptura.*[16]

If the Scriptures are crucial to teaching and learning in the church, and if the liturgy has played a crucial role in maintaining that place for Scripture, would the liturgy be a good place from which to begin thinking about approaches to teaching in the Lutheran church?

Several things commend liturgy as a reference point.

First, the liturgy evolved over a long period of time, making use of the rich tradition of Israel and the church. If during those centuries there was no scientific analysis of learning, there *was* reflection on the nature of humankind and its relationship with God, and this helped to shape the form and content of the liturgy.

Second, the liturgy focuses on the means of grace, the Word and sacraments, which serve as the content and context for teaching/learning in the Lutheran church.

Third, while the liturgy in most Lutheran congregations is expressed in basically fixed forms, it is capable of great variety—for various seasons of the year and times of the day. Taking into account certain essentials, congregations are free to create liturgies for the worship of God. Finally, worship is characteristic of Lutherans, and Lutheran worship uses a particular approach. Although it may not be quite as evident, *teaching* is also characteristic of Lutherans. The approach taken by Lutherans in their teaching, however, may not be, and certainly need not be, as predictable as in their worship. I intend to explore the connections that exist between these two central areas of the church's life, exploring how the liturgy can inform Lutheran approaches to teaching.

There are at least two ways one could proceed in using the liturgy as a reference point in a conversation on approaches to teaching. One is to move progressively through the liturgy itself. While providing a sound structure, it would also lead to repetition. Another is to address the liturgy to those basic questions alluded to earlier, and consider what, if anything, the liturgy could say in response to them. It is this second approach that I have chosen. (The Lutheran liturgy, of course, is not singular. However, I have chosen to build my discussion around the service of Holy Communion.)[17]

Let me point out once again that my intent is only to begin a conversation and point out components of Lutheran approaches to teaching. The continuation of the conversation and the actual formulation of a teaching approach are left to the reader.

The Purpose and Content
of a Lutheran Approach to Teaching

Some time ago I led a session for pastors on the subject of educational objectives. I was arguing for the idea that content should always be determined by objectives. In my presentation I was interrupted by one of the participants who remarked that in the Luthcran tradition the content of faith is so much of our purpose that he could not understand how they could be separated. I think he was, and is, correct. Certainly the content of the liturgy cannot be separated from its purpose.

There is an inescapable relationship between the teaching office of the church and the Scriptures. That being the case, one of the first principles informing an approach to teaching in the Lutheran tradition is that its content informs its purpose as much as purpose determines content. The former seems to run counter to some educational theory, and in doing so marks one of the peculiar features of a Lutheran approach to teaching.

Like teaching, worship is a given for the people of God. Unlike teaching, however, the reformers did not take it for granted. In his explanation to the First Article of the Apostles' Creed, Luther made it clear that worship *is* the appropriate response of those who believe in God the Creator.[18] Worship is the vocation of all Christians. The purpose of the liturgy is to enhance and give direction to that worship. In doing so, the liturgy also gets at two related purposes: affirming the community of faith as the people of God, and challenging these people to be the servants of God in the world. A central purpose of educational ministry is to assist the community of faith to participate in its liturgy. And, not coincidentally, educational ministry shares with the liturgy the two related purposes noted above. At the same time that it provides these key foci for educational ministry, the liturgy also suggests both centers of content and kinds of objectives that could give direction to a Lutheran approach to teaching.

Centers of content

The Scriptures, either directly or indirectly, serve as the content for much of the liturgy. They appear in the liturgy, however, as a series of headlines. It could not be otherwise. Each time the community of faith gathers together for worship, it not only expresses faith, but the *what* of that faith as well. That *what,* presented in abbreviated form in the liturgy, assumes that the worshiper brings to the service a background of knowledge and understanding. A purpose of educational ministry is to provide that background. Some of the key stories in the liturgy that are amplified by educational ministry are the sacraments, the Creed, the Lord's Prayer, and confession and absolution. There is nothing surprising about those centers of content. Every Lutheran recognizes them as the components in Luther's Small Catechism, the content in Lutheran educational efforts second only to the Scriptures. The liturgy centers on the story of God's redeeming act in Jesus Christ, whether that is expressed in the singing of the "Lamb of God," the "Hymn of Praise," the preaching of law and gospel, or the celebration of the sacraments. This center of content is consistent with Paul's teaching (1 Cor. 15:3ff.). Paul's theology of the cross and resurrection are also at the center of Lutheran teaching.

Within the liturgy there is a place where the Scriptures themselves occupy a central place. This comes in the reading of the lessons and the sermon. Both are done for instruction as well as edification. Whenever the Scriptures are read, they fulfill a teaching function. Preachers cannot help but teach when they interpret and speak about their understanding of a text. As Locke Bowman pointed out, however, the hearing of the sermon is dependent on the prior learning of the worshipers. Of necessity, preachers will use biblical material in their sermons. They will refer to basic doctrines of the faith. Knowing the larger stories behind that biblical and doctrinal material enables a richer understanding of, and response to the sermon.[19] It is not surprising that the Bible occupies a central place in the various curriculum materials published by Lutherans.

Kinds of objectives

Worship is enhanced when participants have a larger knowledge and understanding of their faith than what meets them in the headlines of the liturgy. That means that cognitive objectives must be a part of a Lutheran approach to teaching. While this is not the place to discuss connections between learning theory and the liturgy in detail, a few comments illustrate the possible fruitfulness of such an exploration. For example, the liturgy itself represents a marvelous synthesis of the faith of the church. It can also be memorized and analyzed according to its parts. Evaluative thinking would explore the criteria for significant worship and determine appropriate worship for various age groups. All of this dictates that educational efforts designed to enhance worship strive to include in their objectives these various levels of cognitive thinking.[20]

Worship is not simply a cognitive exercise. It is the response of the whole person. In educational terms, that includes the cognitive, the affective, and the behavioral components of learning. Liturgy that allows only the first is a poor structure for worship, and approaches to teaching that do not include the latter two are inadequate as ways of preparing believers to worship.

The affective dimension of the worshiper is addressed in several ways in the liturgy and in the environment where liturgy is done. Musical expression is one of the surest ways to engage the emotions. Organs, pianos, trumpets, and guitars are among the instruments that find a place in worship. Hymns are sung. Bodily actions, such as kneeling, standing, and raising one's arms, evoke feelings. The architectural design of the worship space may contribute to both a sense of the transcendence of God and of God's immediate presence among God's people.

What people know and understand about the liturgy affects how they feel as they participate in it. Knowing they are free from the bondage of sin, they are free to accept themselves and others. Knowing that in Baptism they have been made children of God and initiated into God's family, they can have a sense of belonging and worth. Knowing that the bread and wine in the Lord's Supper are for them, for the forgiveness of sins, encourages and sustains them in their daily walk. And the salutation is a source of assurance that God is with them. All these point to the rich, affective dimension in the liturgy.

Again, worship is an experience that engages the whole person. Whatever approach a Lutheran teacher takes, it must include a significant place for the affective element if students are to be enabled to participate in the liturgy. Students who have not been encouraged and allowed to receive and respond on an affective level to what they see, hear, think, know, understand, and believe may well find worship something of a bore, and they may participate in it on a level similar to that of a fence post.

Educational efforts that include a deliberate concern for the affective not only have an impact on the worship of the community of faith, they also influence how the community sees and responds to the world. Receiving and responding to the joys and sorrows of the world—to its limitations and its possibilities, to its laughter and its pain, to its advantaged and disadvantaged peoples, to its goodness and its injustices—is a matter of the will and values. These, in turn, are in the realm of the affective. Response, of course, leads to action, and that suggests yet a third kind of objective—those that are called *behavioral*.

It may be that because they have not been enabled to participate in the liturgy cognitively and affectively, some who attend worship perceive the liturgy as something to observe—like a spectator sport. For those who know what to look for, who have a sense of the synthesis in the liturgy, and for those who have been enabled to respond to it, it is an experience filled with actions. Those actions are centered around confession, praise, and thanksgiving. Throughout the liturgy, participants are encouraged to act. Not all those actions are kinetic. Reflective thought, arising out of the reading of the texts and the hearing of the sermon, is active too. And action is projected beyond the time the congregation is together in worship. The liturgy concludes: "Go in peace. Serve the Lord." The worshipers respond, "Thanks be to God." In the liturgy the bond between God and God's people has been affirmed. Assured of that bond, worshipers are challenged to love others, wherever they meet them, as they love themselves. The liturgy involves action, is a call to action, and enables the activity of believers.

Even before Jean Piaget, but surely since his research has become known, it was recognized that learning involved the action of the learner. Over the centuries the liturgy has provided that same clue for teachers. It's curious that this clue was overlooked by so many. Today it would hardly seem possible that any approach to teaching would not include in its purposes some targeted behaviors. Those behaviors may be as simple as learning to fold one's hands in prayer, or as complex as struggling to write a paper on the subject of the Trinity. Concern for behavior includes a range from the very personal to world hunger and the threat of nuclear war. The purpose of educational ministry must be to give specificity to these actions and then to provide information, opportunity for the development of skills, and support that enable believers to do them—whether these actions are directly in support of the church's ministries of evangelism, stewardship, teaching, worship, or administration, or in the church's call to struggle in social and justice issues that involve all humankind.

In summary, the liturgy is rich in what it has to offer for our discussion about the purpose and content of educational ministry. Its appeal to the whole person, on a variety of levels, suggests that whatever approach Lutheran teachers use in their teaching, they can do no less.

Context in a Lutheran Approach to Teaching

If the liturgy is its reference point, then it is clear that the community of faith is the context for a Lutheran approach to teaching. The liturgy may be artistically pleasing to some people, or sociologically and psychologically interesting to others, but for those of the household of faith it is most importantly an expression of faith and commitment— first, of God for God's people; and second, of God's people for God. Worship is an act that has profound meaning because of the relationship that exists between worshipers and the one they worship. Whether or not others understand, appreciate, or believe in that dimension of the liturgy makes no difference to the community of faith. Worship remains its vocation. The liturgy has arisen out of that community and now continues to create and shape it through the means of grace. The liturgy and the community that worships through it cannot be separated.

In a similar way the community of faith is the context for the church's educational ministry. In the body of believers one learns, in a variety of ways, the deeper meanings of the sacraments. In the community of faith the Scriptures are recognized and taught as the norm in all areas of faith and morals. In the community of faith one repeatedly hears the assurance of belonging to God and the challenge to be God's people in the world. It is the community of faith that provides the content and purpose for educational ministry—as well as the teachers to carry out that ministry. In sum, a Lutheran approach to teaching assumes the community of faith as the context for educational ministry.

That assumption, however, raises two questions: Is the community of faith the *only* context? If it is, how broadly should it be conceived? From what has been said thus far, one could conclude that the only time there is teaching and learning for Lutherans is when they are gathered either in the sanctuary or in the educational area of the church. While significant learning does happen in those places, neither the community of faith nor teaching/learning are limited to those spheres.

Further discussion of these questions will be facilitated by moving on to yet another question: Who is the teacher in a Lutheran approach to teaching? That question, too, forces yet one more prior question: Who is the learner? After considering both of these, I will return briefly to the matter of the context in a Lutheran approach to teaching.

The Learner in a Lutheran Approach to Teaching

The nature of humankind is clearly presented in the liturgy. As the liturgy begins, participants are led to confess that they are in bondage to sin and cannot free themselves. That bondage means that they cannot think, feel, or act their way into a positive relationship with God. In their whole persons they are sinners. The good news, however, is that God in Christ has set them free. In Baptism they have been made children of God. In the liturgy, participants are assured that though they remain sinners, they are also, by God's grace, saints. Within them is the Holy Spirit—the Spirit that calls, gathers, enlightens, and sanctifies them. The learner is a saint-sinner.

The fact that the learner is a saint-sinner has several implications for an approach to teaching. To begin with, the teacher should realize that there is no innate ability in the learner to come to know and believe in the Lord Jesus Christ. Sinful humanity waits for the initiative of God. Being set free from bondage, God's purpose in sending Jesus into the world, is not accomplished through educational efforts but by God's saving acts. Faith in this saving act, like the act itself, is a gift of God. Whatever approach teachers take, both teachers and learners must wait on the Lord for the giving of the gift. This waiting does not imply that teachers have nothing to do. God has given the means of grace and the fellowship of believers and commanded that the church teach.

While learners are sinners, they are also saints. While never escaping their sinful natures, they have been given a great capacity for learning and doing good. It is no compliment to God's grace to have low—or no—expectations of God's redeemed people. In fact, it is no compliment to God's creation to have a low expectation level of people in general. Outside of salvation, and within the confession of God the Creator, humankind has a capacity to learn beyond our present ability to measure. Approaches to teaching in the Lutheran tradition must allow for both that creative, and recreated, capacity that God has given.

Learning is a human activity assisted by people called teachers. The emphasis in education on the human element may make it suspect in a church that overemphasizes the sinner aspect of the human condition. It could even be a reason for subordinating teaching to preaching and the sacraments to such an extent that teaching loses its supportive function for those activities. If that were the case, there would be all the more reason to stress the importance of creation, and recreation— along with the reality of the learner as sinner *and* saint—in a Lutheran approach to teaching.

The Teacher in a Lutheran Approach to Teaching

The liturgy begins with the invocation in the name of the Triune God. It concludes with either the benediction or, "Thanks be to God." Throughout, the liturgy communicates the conviction that God is the initiator and enabler of the relationship that exists between God and God's people. Word and sacraments are the revealers of that initiative. There, in the final analysis, are the teaching authorities—and yes, the teacher—of the community of faith. In bondage to sin, humankind cannot come to God. God came, and continues to come, to teach God's people through the means God has chosen and given. At the center of those means of grace is the gospel, and at the core of the gospel is Jesus Christ. Those called to teach in the church have derived their authority from their submission and commitment to Jesus.

While that teaching is often done in space set aside for that purpose, no space is excluded from serving as a teaching context. The Word and sacraments come to hospitals, homes, places of business, camps, battlefields—wherever the faithful are gathered or represented. The Word may be read, heard, and reflected on in more situations than we can imagine. The force and truth of the Word and sacraments can be discovered in life situations that run the full gamut of human experience. The immediate teacher may be a book, a person, or an event. God's Spirit blows where it will. Where it does, there are those who are taught—and who learn.

While centering on the gospel and the means of grace, the liturgy does not limit God's revelation to them. God is the Creator of the heavens and the earth. All things come from God and, for the faithful, have the potential to teach. And in this world that God created there is so much to learn: chemistry, biology, political science, languages— the list could go on and on. Persons don't have to be members of the community of faith to teach these, and members of that community don't have to fear learning from them. Laboratories, classrooms, inner cities, wilderness areas, courtrooms, operating rooms, streets, and sidewalks—all are contexts for learning for the people of faith, and in their own way may serve as teachers.

At the same time, all these learning experiences need reflection and interpretation. Significant places in which to do this, places to which one can bring them, are worship and the class, where deliberate efforts are made to connect these experiences with the revelation of God in the Word and sacraments. At this point one again returns to the teacher as one who is called to teach—to teach in submission to the revelation of God in Jesus Christ.

In a Lutheran approach to teaching the teacher is both narrowly and broadly conceived. Because of human limitations, the essential teacher is revelation, especially God's revelation in Jesus Christ. Teachers in the community of faith derive their authority through submission to the revelation. In a broader sense, however, all creation bears witness to God. And because it does, it simply is not possible to limit the ways through which human beings learn. A Lutheran approach to teaching would allow for these and respect and incorporate them as the gospel is brought to their interpretation and understanding. Certainly, in a Lutheran approach to teaching, no single human teacher can ever assume that he or she can, or should, teach all there is to teach. Still, the urgency of the gospel commends to every human teacher the need to bring all things to the center of that gospel—Jesus Christ, the one who has taught, as has none other, the love and mercy of God.

Methods in a Lutheran Approach to Teaching

In taking their first teacher-education course, some come with the expectation that they will be shown the "tricks of the trade" that will enable them to be teachers. Like Thomas Hardy's Jude, who found that there was no easy way to learn Latin and Greek, these would-be teachers are bound to be disappointed. One of my professors in graduate school grew upset when his students criticized him for spending too much time on the foundations of education and too little on methods. "All they want is gimmicks," he would complain, "and they aren't concerned for the real stuff that makes a teacher." In a way his complaint was justified. Teaching is more than methods. Teachers should choose methods after reflecting on all the areas that have been included thus far in this discussion. On the other hand, methods are what students experience. Methods are both the evidence for, and the conclusion of, what teachers think, value, and strive for in their teaching. Methods are the observable level of the teacher's approach; therefore teachers must pay careful attention to them.

While methods are a crucial concern for teaching, can the same be said of them in the liturgy? Indeed, does the liturgy make use of methods? The answer to both, I think, is yes—especially if methods are seen as ways of achieving a designated purpose. In the case of the liturgy, the purpose is worship. Though *method* may not be the best word to describe how the liturgy goes about achieving that purpose, it does make use of a variety of "ways." There are several things that can be said about these ways or methods.

They are varied. Music is one component of most liturgies, but not just any music will do. Hymns are chosen to reflect the theme of a particular season of the church year and the sense of the texts and the sermon. Organ, piano, and instrumental music provide preludes, postludes, and offertories that elicit a variety of affective and cognitive responses. Music at a Christmas Eve candlelight service is different from that of a Sunday morning communion service, and both are likely to be different from that of a youth service held at a weekend retreat.

At various places in the liturgy there is prayer. Again, as in the case of music, prayers are varied in their content—and sometimes call for a response from the congregation. Still other methods used in the liturgy are the reading of the Scriptures, the sermon, the confession of faith, the use of responsive readings and liturgical dance, the giving of offerings, the sharing of the peace, and silence.

They take into account all of the senses. Early on in the Reformation Luther decided to keep that part of the Roman Catholic tradition that in his judgment did not violate Scripture. That meant, for Lutherans, keeping a feast for the eyes in their worship setting. Whether worship is experienced in a space especially constructed for that purpose or not, the worship leader can do much to arrange the setting so that worship is enriched by what participants see. Music and the spoken word fill the ears of worshipers as they participate in the liturgy. The touch of hands, the feel of water, and the taste of bread and wine appeal to the senses of taste and touch. Even the sense of smell may be appealed to in the liturgy—through the scent of flowers, incense, or whatever becomes identified with a particular place of worship.

They allow for a variety of actions. At first glance the liturgy doesn't seem to provide much opportunity for action. A more careful look, however, dispels that notion. The leader, the choir, the ushers, the acolytes, and the lectors are all active in the liturgy. In addition, all participants are invited to be active in the *singing* of the hymns, in *stating* their confession of faith, in *making* the sign of the cross, in *kneeling,* in *coming* to the altar for the sacrament, in *taking* the bread and wine, in *sharing* the peace, and in *praying.* In addition, opportunity is given for *reflecting* on the sermon and the reading of the texts. Participants in worship are not expected to be passive.

They are dialogical. The liturgy is an ongoing dialog—between God and the community of faith, and between the leader and the participants. The Kyrie, the prayer petitions, and the salutations are obvious indications of that dialog. They point to the basic tone of the liturgy—that of receiving and responding, confessing and absolving, listening-act-ing-listening, and believing.

Research into learning has had an impact on the concern for ap-proaches to teaching—and the methods used in those approaches. Had teachers of the church been more sensitive to methods in the liturgy, which they experienced weekly, they might have discovered genera-tions ago what has become commonplace in educational practice today. The liturgy had its sermon, but it had so much more. How, then, could classes have lectures—and only lectures?

Educational methods are *almost* infinite in number. This chapter suggests some guidelines for the use of methods in a Lutheran approach to teaching: methods should be varied; they should involve as many senses of the learner as possible; they should allow for the activity of the learner; and they should be dialogical.

One more thing needs to be said with respect to this last point. David Silvernail, in *Teaching Styles as Related to Student Achievement,* has suggested that there are two basic styles of teaching. He named them the *direct* and *indirect* styles. In the direct style, teaching methods stress information and the authority of the teacher. In the indirect style, the ideas and participation of students are emphasized. He claims that research shows that neither approach is necessarily better than the other. Their use is dependent on the structure and objectives of the class. When they are used in mutually supportive ways, learning is positively affected.[21]

Some teachers tend to identify with one or the other of these styles. There are those who want their classes to be rich in content, and who assume an authoritative role in presenting that content. Others see themselves as enablers. Concerned with process and the needs of stu-dents, they may hesitate to use any methods that suggest an authoritative position in the classroom—for example, a lecture.

In those sections of this chapter dealing with the purpose, the content, the teacher, and the student in a Lutheran approach to teaching, I have tried to support Silvernail's conclusions. Methods appropriate to both styles belong in a Lutheran approach to teaching. The Scriptures are authoritative for the church. Our bondage to sin makes it impossible for us to discover Christ or believe in him. Because of God's revelation and our need for it, there must be an authoritative communication of revelation and methods that make the communication effective. On the other hand, teachers are challenged to interpret and understand that revelation, and to help others do the same. This requires a more indirect approach and appropriate methods.

In the liturgy the direct style is more dominant. In educational ministry there is the possibility and need for greater balance. In any case, there is no doubt that both are present in the former, and the presence of both should be a significant characteristic of a Lutheran approach to teaching.

Evaluation in a Lutheran Approach to Teaching

While differing on how it should be done, and who and what should be its object, educators in general agree that evaluation is integral to any approach to teaching.

Many religious educators are not so sure.[22] Some argue that religious convictions are of such a personal nature that they cannot be evaluated by another. Others claim that there is no way of measuring faith, and since faith can't be measured, why evaluate anything? A few claim that evaluation is presumptuous—an attempt to make judgments of God, who alone is the author and finisher of faith. If these are questions that can be raised as objections to the use of evaluation in educational ministry, couldn't one anticipate finding even more objections to its use in the liturgy? Or, put in another way, is there any evidence of evaluation in the liturgy? Interestingly enough, there is. And, that evaluation is expressed in what some educators might find most distasteful in evaluation—the making of judgments. Of course, the judgments have to be personally applied, but they are there.

The sermon is one place where this evaluation may appear. In the preaching of the law and gospel hearers may sense that they are under judgment—or conversely, have a gospel-based freedom from judgment. The singing of hymns may provide another source for judgment. Whether the sermon or the hymns ever communicate the words of judgment or release, however, the liturgy still assures that they will be heard. They are inherent in the Office of the Keys, confession and absolution. To those who repent, the announcement is made that their sins are forgiven. For those who do not repent, the opposite word is spoken. They are still in their sins and under the judgment of God.

As any teacher knows, evaluation has many sides. Even as students are being evaluated, they are drawing conclusions about what they are learning, how they are learning it, and the teachers who are there to help them learn. The same can be said for the liturgy. As they worship, the people who are the church make judgments about themselves. They make judgments about the hymns they sing, the pace of the liturgy, the sermon, the length of the service, the poise and effectiveness of the worship leader, and the space where they are worshiping. As a result of their evaluation, some people leave the Lutheran church to join a so-called nonliturgical church. Others join the Lutheran church because they value its liturgy. Most members of the Lutheran church make comments from time to time about their appreciation, or the lack of it, for the way they worship. The comments and actions alluded to above are, in their own way, forms of evaluation.

Since evaluation of a sort seems to be a functioning aspect of the church, it makes sense that it be done well. In fact, evaluation is a way of adding value to whatever is its object. As George admitted to Emily in Thornton Wilder's *Our Town,* people don't bother to make judgments about people or things they don't care about. The earlier section on purpose mentioned evaluative thinking. According to Benjamin Bloom, several questions are involved in evaluative thinking: What is the purpose of whatever is being evaluated? What are the criteria by which the evaluation can be made? Having applied the criteria, what judgments can be made?

At least one purpose for the liturgy is to provide a way for the people of God to worship the one in whom they believe. While leaders in the field of liturgical studies can offer criteria for measuring how well any particular liturgy carries out that purpose, individuals and congregations can do the same. Those criteria are likely to fall into three categories: the liturgy itself, the presider, and, the participation of the worshipers. Sample criteria for each category might be:

The Liturgy
1. Is the liturgy consistent with the expressed faith of the worshiping community?

2. Does the liturgy have present and future dimensions, as well as those of the past?

The Presider
1. Does the presider bring life to the liturgy?
2. Is the presider (and preacher) prepared and able to engage the congregation in the liturgy and sermon?

The Worshipers
1. Does the congregation understand the liturgy well enough to participate in it meaningfully?
2. Is there enthusiasm in the congregation's participation in the liturgy?

Coming to conclusions as a result of the application of evaluative criteria need not be a negative experience. In fact, it ought not to be. Any evaluative exercise should result in finding something to be *affirmed*. And when evaluation points out areas for change, that should not be a big problem—not if one is motivated toward a fuller realization of purpose.

Evaluation *is* present in the liturgy. Since it is there, it should be done well. Now, if evaluation finds a place in the liturgy, it only makes sense that it should be a part of a Lutheran approach to teaching. Those judgments include a concern for what the church "believes and teaches" and how faithfully it reflects those teachings.

In addition, evaluation in educational ministry is one of the surest ways leading to the improvement of instruction, to improved teaching performance, to greater student learning, and to the overall enrichment of an educational program. A Lutheran approach to teaching would include evaluation as one of its dimensions.

The Liturgy and a Lutheran Approach to Teaching

Using the ideas I have suggested as a place to start, and the freedom and responsibility that each teacher has, teachers are challenged to construct their own approaches to teaching. (Personally, I am drawn to Groome's shared praxis approach. Any approach, however, that includes the dimensions of action, reflection, communication, and dialog would interest me.)

In conclusion, I would add three more thoughts about the liturgy and teaching.

First, the liturgy is done. Perhaps the most predictable aspect of the church's life is that it worships, and when it does, the liturgy is done. One could hope that teaching, along the lines of a lifelong catechumenate, would be equally predictable in the life of the church, and that this teaching would reflect some of the same intuitive sense that is present in the liturgy.

Second, much that is intuitive in the liturgy is now considered good teaching/learning theory for education. It is interesting to speculate as to why those insights weren't more readily applied to teaching in the church generations ago. It would be even more curious if the church were not to implement those insights today in its teaching ministry, now that contemporary theory has come along to support them.

Third, the liturgy does, and teaching/learning experiences should, end in a spirit of mystery. Teachers are called to help their students as they struggle to understand their faith. However successful that struggle, it finally should end in wonder, awe, and praise—at least it should if the teacher's approach is Lutheran.

TEN

ADMINISTRATION OF CHRISTIAN EDUCATION

Mary E. Hughes

Administration has a bad reputation. Some people say, "I don't like all that paperwork. I would rather work with people. Details drive me crazy." If this was what administration was all about, few people would choose to be administrators. However, there is more to administration than paperwork, and most of it deals directly with people and with helping them use their gifts more effectively.

This chapter will examine five functions of administration of Christian education in a congregation. Although they will differ from congregation to congregation and person to person, each of those functions is a part of administration.

Several principles underlie the understanding of administration basic to this chapter:

1. The word *administration* is based on the word *minister*. The Latin root means "to serve." Administration is itself ministry, and it enables others to minister more effectively. God's people have received a host of gifts. Administration helps identify those gifts and enables people to use them to build up the whole body of Christ.

2. Administration has to do with people and ministry to them, with them, and for them. Reports, forms, numbers, catalogs, and charts can be valuable, but their purpose is to help ministry happen. For instance, attendance records focus our attention on those who are absent so that

we can seek them out, remember them in prayer, and invite them to return to our midst.

3. Many persons, but not all, have the gifts and opportunity to be administrators. The people of God have been given many gifts to be used in God's name, and although those gifts may differ, all are to be honored and used with joy. Administrators are not better than or less than any other servants of God. Church administration is not a hierarchical structure in which some ministries are more important than others; all ministries are focused on sharing and living the good news of Jesus Christ.

Administration is a complex topic, but this chapter will discuss five components of the administration of Christian education:

1. the representative function;
2. the information-processing function;
3. the staffing function;
4. the resourcing function;
5. the decision-making function.

The Representative Function of Christian Education

Administration

When a church council appoints a Christian-education committee or when that committee selects other administrators to oversee and implement some portion of education ministry, those administrators are more than individuals working on a task. Those administrators represent Christian education within the congregation. In formal ways the person who coordinates caregiving to infants and toddlers is a symbol and spokesperson for that ministry. The chairperson of the Christian education committee may represent or designate someone else to represent educational ministries when budgets are being discussed and decisions made. The Sunday school superintendent represents the entire Sunday school. The director of the vacation school may be the "up-front" person at a special event.

Administrators also represent the congregation within the community and wider church. When area churches jointly sponsor a vacation school, each church's coordinator represents the ministry of her or his entire congregation in the discussions.

In a less formal way, the administrator, as representative, is often the person to whom suggestions, complaints, and questions are directed, because that person is the most visible symbol of the program. Administrators often find this role particularly uncomfortable and difficult, because we often hear complaints as personal criticism and receive suggestions as a sign that we are not doing a good job.

Another aspect of this representative function is making educational ministries known and understood in the congregation and community. Administration can take the initiative and actively seek ways to keep Christian education visible and, thereby, help create a climate in which education is cherished and supported. Some people refer to this as "public relations" but whatever the label, it is important that Christian education be represented well throughout the life of the church.

Clues for implementation

● When others ask questions or offer criticism, listen carefully and seek to understand their concerns. Defensiveness is natural, but not helpful. Perhaps sharing those concerns with a trusted colleague can help objectify the criticism and reduce the tendency to take personal offense at programmatic suggestions.

● Determine a number of ways to inform the congregation and community about Christian education to make it a highly visible ministry. Make it visible in bulletin boards, in newsletters, in brochures describing programs to visitors, in the budget, in informal conversations, and in congregational discussions.

The Information-Processing Function of Christian Education

Administration

Administration is the nerve center that constantly receives and sends information. The Sunday school superintendent hears a concern of the teacher, observes the attendance patterns of preschoolers, listens to a parent, reads about a new filmstrip, and hears the dreams of the Christian education committee. No one else is in the position to receive such broad information regarding the Sunday school. That information comes from the teachers, students, and all those involved in the Sunday school; it comes from the supervising body (in this case, the Christian education committee); and it comes from such sources as Sunday school leaders of other churches, from written publications, from congregational individuals, and persons outside the Sunday school. Information includes not only facts, but also the feelings and attitudes present. Sometimes a sensitivity to the emotional climate is more valuable than facts and figures. All other administrators are similar nerve centers with their own sources of information.

What does one do with all this information? The administrator uses it to maintain an overall picture of the program, to provide data for reports and articles, and to help answer questions. He or she also uses it to determine needs to be met, problems to be addressed, opportunities for affirmation and strengthening. Having all this information, the administrator as spokesperson is in a better position to speak accurately and with insight about the program. The administrator uses this broad knowledge to help make decisions most useful for everyone.

Much of the information an administrator receives is communicated to others: to teachers, to the congregation, or to a committee. Some of it helps predict opportunities and problems or helps give perspective to otherwise unrelated events.

The administrator is a liaison among all those related to the organization or program. She or he needs up-to-date information in order to keep others informed and to make responsible decisions.

Clues for implementation

• Identify all the sources of information available to you as an administrator. What reports, records, periodicals, groups, and individuals can help provide an accurate factual and emotional description of the program?

• Become an active information gatherer rather than a passive one. Engage others in conversations, ask questions, visit and observe, look for opportunities to see and hear more about the program.

The Staffing Function
of Christian Education Administration

Administration is a people business. Administration seeks to engage people in ministry in effective ways and enable them to use God's gifts in building up the body of Christ. Whether seeking a librarian, teachers for Vacation school, members of a committee or planning group, a coordinator of a series of Bible studies, an adult leader of the youth organization, or a superintendent of Sunday school, staffing involves identifying, recruiting, supporting, and recognizing persons in ministry.

Identification

Whom should we ask to do this? Who will decide? On what basis will we decide? What ministries are already happening, and who is now engaged in those ministries?

Identifying persons for ministry involves recognizing gifts and strengths of one another and encouraging people to use them in appropriate ministries. Perhaps we see qualities in a person that suggest they would relate to young children in a caring way or that their organizational abilities would be valuable in planning a project. Part of identifying personnel is naming one another's gifts—naming those gifts to that person and offering them a way to use those gifts.

In seeking to identify both the ministries and the persons who might engage in them, we sometimes overlook the ministries that occur every day. The person providing transportation to a children's choir program or helping prepare meals on a youth retreat may not use the word *ministry* to describe their activity. It is important to name these and other ministries, as well as naming the gifts that are being used.

Identifying persons who will be asked to serve in any way—teacher, committee member, or group leader—is not the task of a single person. In fact, a small group will have greater knowledge of the congregation than any one person. Teachers are sometimes recruited by one or two persons after the entire Christian education committee (or a planning group) has prayerfully considered and developed a list of persons to approach.

Recruitment

How will we ask them to do recruitment? To recruit someone is to issue an invitation to engage in a specific ministry for a specific reason: "A need or an opportunity has been identified. We believe that you have certain gifts to bring to this situation, and we would like for you to consider sharing yourself in this way." Too often prospective teachers are approached apologetically: "We know you're too busy, but this won't take much time, and we really need to get someone to teach this class." Why should someone accept this invitation? We are inviting persons to engage in an exciting and important ministry, one that needs and deserves the time and energy it will require. Persons wish to be part of activities that are valued, and if the church values its educational ministry, we can enthusiastically invite them to become a part of that ministry.

Clues for recruitment

• Recruit staff in person, face-to-face, in a setting that is not distracting or hurried.

• Be clear about why you are asking this person to do this work. What gifts and strengths make them a right choice for this position?

• Know exactly what you are asking them to do and for what length of time you are asking. Know enough details so that you can describe it to them adequately and can answer their questions. Consider a written "job description" that would include both expectations of them and the support they can expect from others.

• Help them know why this work is important. Share with them the congregation's vision for Christian education, your understanding of its purpose, and how this work fits into that vision. You are asking them to do something important, so let them know that it is worthwhile.

Support

Staffing does not end when a person says, "Yes, I'll do that." It takes a lot of support to ensure that their work is effective and enjoyable. Too often the administration helps those who serve to fail, because the necessary support in terms of orientation, training, resources, organization, feedback, evaluation, and encouragement was insufficient.

An important role of the administrator is to provide ways to ensure the success of those engaged in educational ministries.

Support also includes helping persons leave those positions in which there was a poor match between gifts and ministry. This may be one of the hardest tasks of an administrator and should happen only after careful consideration and discussion with appropriate colleagues. However, there are times when it will be most supportive to either the person giving or those receiving, or both, for an individual to be replaced by one whose gifts can be more effectively used in this particular ministry.

Clues for supporting those who serve

• Plan ways for these persons to prepare for their work and to continue to improve while doing it. Identify written resources, workshops, and people who can help train the new vacation school director, the children's choir director, the youth group leaders, and all who accept responsibilities in ministry. Let regular meetings of teachers or committees become educational and inspirational as well as informational.

• Provide adequate materials at the right time.

• Provide helpful feedback and evaluation. There is no need to overwhelm a person with negatives, but a conversation in which several strengths are affirmed and one point for improvement is identified can be useful and appreciated when done thoughtfully.

• Help create in the congregation a climate that values what these persons are doing. Why should persons give their time and energy to something about which other people do not care? Often the best support that can be given is the recognition that they are involved in something we think is important.

• Help those who serve know they are part of the whole team of educational ministry. Provide opportunities when groups can share together and get to know one another as partners and resources.

• Help persons who serve to maintain a sense of the importance of their work and a knowledge of forgiveness in their humanness.

• Actively listen to their joys and their complaints, and remember them often in your prayers.

Recognition

The question is not whether we will give recognition to persons engaged in ministry in our congregations, but to which persons and in what ways will we give that recognition? In most congregations the ministries of some persons are highly visible, frequently mentioned, and sometimes formally recognized. Some names appear in bulletins and newsletters; some receive certificates or have a banquet in their honor. Other persons engaged in ministry may never be noticed. Planning groups and committees are seldom thanked. Sunday morning teachers often arrive before others, spend their time with their class or study group, and must then hurry to get to worship, but the congregation may not even know the names of these teachers, because their preparation is done alone and at home and their work is carried out with a small group in an isolated classroom. To give recognition inconsistently is a common, but demoralizing, practice. It is essential that the ministry of those engaged in educational ministry be recognized.

Clues for recognition

● Publicly call attention to the programs in which these persons are involved: tell the congregation about the catechetical instruction, post pictures from the adult Bible-study group, create a bulletin board about the marriage-enrichment series, list the new books received in the library. By recognizing the programs, the leaders are recognized.

● Plan a service of commitment or affirmation when persons begin or continue their ministries—not just for some, but for all educational leaders and whenever appropriate.

● Find ways throughout the year to affirm these educational leaders both formally and informally: a personal note, appreciation dinners, an "educator of the week" column in the newsletter, pictures of committee members on the bulletin board, a personal conversation or telephone call.

● As persons conclude a time of service, sit down with them for an "exit interview." Ask them to reflect on the ministry in which they were engaged—its ups and downs, their times of satisfaction, and their hopes for the future. Hear their advice and ideas for continuing that ministry. This affirms their ministry, helps them to be part of furthering that program, and helps us strengthen existing programs.

The staffing function of Christian education also includes the continual development of educational leadership. Even when there is no immediate need for additional teachers or other leaders, it is important to constantly identify those whose gifts may match educational ministries, encourage them to become involved, and provide them opportunities to prepare for and engage in those ministries.

The Resourcing Function of Christian Education Administration

Resources include buildings and furnishings, physical space, time, money, human energy, supplies and materials, media, events, people, and curricular materials. One role of administration is to decide which of the church's resources will be used and how they will be used. Organizing the congregation's educational ministry in coordination with other community and church ministries so that they are used most faithfully requires sensitive stewardship.

What criteria will be used to determine the use of resources? The selection and use of resources should be (1) theologically sound, that is, consistent with the doctrine of the church; (2) appropriate to the local situation, that is, appropriate for our size, our setting, our purposes, our uniqueness; and (3) appropriate for these persons, that is, usable by our teachers and our students, our planners and administrators.

One of the resourcing decisions to be made is selection of printed curriculum materials for use in educational settings. The term *curriculum* has many definitions and often refers to a broad plan for education. However, in this chapter *curriculum* refers to those books, media, student packets, and other materials published for study use.

There is no perfect curriculum. When there are problems, dissatisfaction, or simply boredom, curriculum is often blamed, and a change in curriculum is made. But changing curriculum does not guarantee change in results. Unless helped to change, persons teach the same way regardless of the materials. In this case, after brief satisfaction with new curriculum, the same old problems will recur, curriculum will be blamed, and the real sources of the problems will not be addressed.

Although there is no perfect curriculum, some will be a "better fit" than others. The goal is to find the resources that are the most appropriate for your congregation, while realizing that curriculum is only one aspect of the teaching and learning adventure.

The following steps in evaluating and selecting curriculum materials may be completed over many weeks or concentrated into a few sessions.

1. Review the present Christian education program in your church: organization, size of classes, teachers, and materials now being used.

2. Review your understanding of the goals and purpose of Christian education and the basic doctrine that permeates ministry, including educational ministry.

3. Discuss with each teacher the strengths and weaknesses of the curriculum now being used. Talk with some parents and students and any others affected by the curriculum.

4. Determine the criteria by which curricula will be evaluated, so that all materials are being judged by the same standards (see "Criteria for Examining Curriculum" at the end of this chapter).

5. Critique a variety of curriculum resources in light of the criteria.

6. Review the results of your critique and determine action to be taken: continue current resources, modify use of current resources, or change curriculum.

7. Report the results to all the appropriate persons and groups.

Clues for curriculum evaluation and selection

● Curriculum choice is not a decision for one person; it involves the Christian education committee, teachers, parents, students, and other staff.

● Evaluate materials firsthand by asking for examination copies or samples. A local resource center or nearby church may loan them for examination, a local bookstore may obtain the materials, and publishers will often send materials for review on request.

● Denominational publishers are responsible and accountable to provide materials theologically consistent with their church's teachings.

Independent publishers have a particular theological orientation, but are not held accountable by any church body. It is important to evaluate material's theological content before using it in your own congregation.

There are other important resource-related decisions. Administration includes making sure that the available resources are really accessible and usable. For instance, does the schedule allow the time needed for classes and groups to function well? Are events coordinated so that the best space is used effectively? Is the physical environment attractive and inviting? If more than one group uses the same room, are provisions made for each to have space that fits its needs? Do leaders know how to find and use the projectors, record players, filmstrips, and supplies? Is equipment kept in good repair? Are there adequate finances to provide the resources needed? Educational administrators can often coordinate their plans and needs with other church leaders to insure that resources are used to greatest benefit in ministry.

The Decision-making Function of Christian Education

Administration

Decision making is a constant part of a leader's work. Some of those decisions will concern immediate problems or opportunities. However, most decisions do not actually involve crises. There is usually time to review and gather the needed information, consider several alternatives and their outcomes, select one of the alternatives, and implement it. Other decisions are more long-term, involve greater planning and goal setting, and may allow for more creativity and innovation.

Administration's information-processing function plays an important part in decision making. Having broad information makes responsible decision making possible. Decision making about curriculum choice has already been discussed. Another critical aspect of decision making centers around planning.

The most common planning process is very simple to describe: compare the present situation with the preferred situation and identify ways to help move from the present to the preferred. It sounds simple, but each step is complex:

1. What is the preferred situation? What is our ideal, our vision? Describing the ideal requires work. Articulating one's vision for the

youth group, the adult study program, catechetics, the youth choir, the women's organization, confirmation ministry, or for Christian education as a whole will involve study, discussion, and hard work.

2. What is the present situation? How can we describe ourselves in facts and figures, in values and commitment? How shall we describe our strengths and weaknesses, our potential and our limitations?

3. How does the present and the potential compare with the ideal and preferred? This comparison, this evaluation, leads to goal setting: identifying the ends or broad objectives toward which you or your group will work.

4. How will you achieve those goals? In this strategizing various ideas for action are identified and considered, and from those alternatives a plan is eventually designed and implemented.

This general framework of planning can apply to looking at the next 10 years in Christian education at one's church or to looking at ways to respond more faithfully to a gifted child in the seventh-grade catechetical program.

In their book *Creative Church Administration,* Schaller and Tidwell discuss planning from weakness and planning from strength. To identify that area in which we are functioning most poorly and to make it our highest priority may be planning from weakness. If it has been our weakest area, it is likely that neither the resources nor the interest is present to improve it dramatically. However, by identifying our greatest needs and our particular strengths and resources, we can plan from strength—that is, determine how our unique gifts can be used to meet needs.

The planning process, however, is not neat and tidy. Although it can be described in logical steps, all these steps may constantly be happening. Some of the most creative dreaming, most effective visioning, or most useful strategizing may happen in informal discussions following a meeting rather than during the group's brainstorming. The more formal planning process, however, allows all group members to share in planning and decision making, and this may bring greater creativity to the process and strengthen the results because of a broader base of support.

Clues for planning

● An important question to ask when describing the present is, How did this come to be this way? By asking questions of tradition and history, the planners respect work of the past and gain insights for the future.

● Decisions and decision making reflect theology. Budgets arc theological statements of values. The name given to a new fellowship room, the permission given or withheld to use the building, the invitations to the community to vacation school—all these decisions require theological consideration. What theological message is given in each decision you make?

● In decision making, seek group consensus rather than a vote. Voting implies that some people won and some people lost. It is more important to come to a mutual decision that everyone can support than to make quick decisions by voting. Reaching a consensus means that all points of view are discussed openly and explored; then the group comes to a decision that seems best for the group. Not everyone may feel that the decision is best for each individual, but the decision can be supported by all as best for the group as a whole. An important role of the administrator leading the decision-making process is focusing the discussion and helping the group articulate the decision that is being made. Sensitivity to the diversity within a group can lead to richer discussions and more valuable decisions.

● Planning is time consuming. However, the time involved allows for creativity and dreaming, which strengthens the final result.

● There are no perfect decisions. Although administrators must always work toward the ideal, the question is really this: in this situation, with these resources, these dreams, and these limitations, what is the most faithful decision that can be made?

Who Are the Administrators?

Regardless of size, every congregation has administrators in Christian education. A church's constitution usually provides for a Christian education committee to be the primary administrative body, which in turn reports to the church council. The Christian education committee may be large or small, may be divided into subcommittees or task forces, may delegate much of its authority or may retain it. That committee, however, bears the responsibility for administration. The Christian education committee establishes the organizational framework for education ministry within the congregation and coordinates its various components, determines the overall goals for education, and recruits administrators for particular education programs.

These program administrators, or managers, may be called "directors" or "superintendents" or "coordinators," but regardless of title, they see that the goals and purposes established by the committee are implemented in such programs as the Sunday school, vacation school, youth groups, catechetical instruction, women's and men's organizations, adult study programs, and intergenerational ministries.

The pastor also shares administrative responsibilities with the committee, and, in some congregations, directors of Christian education or directors of youth ministry are staff persons with specific responsibilities in educational ministry.

Every congregation has administrators, and, regardless of the scope of their responsibilities, their role will include representative, information processing, staffing, resourcing, and decision-making functions.

Criteria for Examining Curriculum

Name of curriculum _____   Publisher _____
Stated purpose or goals of this curriculum:

Theological considerations

1. How consistent is the material with Lutheran doctrine? Consider concepts such as justification by grace through faith, understanding of the sacraments, understanding of the church, prayer, worship.
2. In what ways is the Bible used and understood in the material?
3. How is attention given to social and global issues?

Educational considerations

1. Are objectives clearly stated, and are the activities appropriate to the objectives?

2. How appropriate are the concepts and activities for the developmental level intended?
3. Is there good variety in teaching/learning activities and styles?
4. What helps are provided for the teacher in preparing and leading the study?

Other considerations

1. How well does it relate to the life needs and concerns of learners?
2. How is it inclusive of gender, cultures, ages, family patterns, and socio-economic status?
3. Does it seem to fit this congregation's situation and setting?
4. Is it attractive?
5. Is it reasonably priced?
6. Is it liked by our teachers?
7. What modifications or preparations would be needed to implement this curriculum in our congregation?

ELEVEN

LEADERSHIP IN CHRISTIAN EDUCATION

Harold F. Park

"Leadership is the key."

"We've always needed to get more leaders."

"The way to have good leaders is to develop them."

"The pastor is a leader in the educational program, either helping it or hurting it."

"Leaders are born *and* made."

All of the above statements are true. One-half million women and men are serving as Christian education leaders in Lutheran congregations, as committee members, church school directors, youth group advisers, pastors, auxiliary officers, and teachers. Leadership is already happening in every congregation and is vital. Since the quality of leadership is crucial for carrying out the mission of the congregation, it is important to understand how leadership operates and to help leaders function more effectively.

Leadership is not the prerogative of a few dynamic individuals. It is a dimension of each Christian's response to God as responsible stewardship of the manifold gifts of grace, exercised in relationships with other persons and in active participation in the mission of the church. In this sense leadership is a ministry of everyone in the priesthood of believers. Some of these persons are assigned specific tasks and identified with designated positions, such as Sunday school superintendent or librarian. However, leadership should not be thought of as positions or as status, but as functions and activities to be lived and done between and among workers.

Definition of Leadership

The literature in management, systems, and church administration provides various definitions of leadership, but most describe leadership as the activity or process involving interaction and influence with persons, leading toward goal accomplishment, and usually resulting in some form of changed behavior or structure.[1] Since leadership involves accomplishing goals with and through persons, a leader must be concerned about tasks and human relationships.[2]

Leadership in Christian education is servant ministry, people serving God by interacting with others to enable educational activity and to enable the church to manifest its nature as the body of Christ and fulfill its mission.

There are no shortcuts or gimmicks or user-friendly computer software to improve leadership, because leadership is persons interacting with other persons, influencing and enabling them to achieve group goals. However, there are many helpful resources based on extensive studies and research in leadership theories, leadership/management styles, organizational systems, motivation, group dynamics, and human relations. Some of these are general studies, related to business or educational organizations with insights applicable to the church, and some are specifically church related. Leadership is usually included in studies of administration and management, although a few studies make distinctions among these. Congregational leaders should make use of the many available print and video resources and workshops in order to understand the leadership dynamics and behaviors that are experienced in the congregation and to work for improvement.

Leadership Functions

The current emphasis in leadership studies is on a functional approach, considering both the individual and the situation in which leadership occurs, and the functions of group members that aid it in accomplishing the group's purposes. Leadership functions may be performed by a designated officer or by many members of the group, such as students in a class.

Some of the leadership functions done by persons involved in Christian education are summarized in five groups:

Initiating: thinking, gathering information, studying, visioning, clarifying objectives, seeing and building connections, proposing ideas and agendas.

Planning: goal setting, considering alternatives, making decisions, prioritizing time and activities.

Managing: maintaining the organization, implementing, directing, delegating, coordinating, communicating, recruiting, and developing leaders and participants.

Supervising: listening, inspiring, observing, assisting, providing resources and training, supporting, enabling and empowering, analyzing.

Improving: being accountable, evaluating process and goals and results, identifying tensions and conflicts, solving problems, referring, consulting, making changes, and continuing.

From the above it is obvious that leadership in Christian education involves *both* task functions and human relationship (or maintenance) functions. Task functions focus primarily on getting particular jobs done, such as recruiting a kindergarten teacher, ordering and distributing literature, planning a Christmas pageant, or writing and filing an evaluation of the recent vacation school. Human relationship functions focus primarily on the persons involved and the group itself, such as encouraging youth officers to take more initiative and responsibility, showing care and concern for a teacher and not merely for his or her task, helping committee members to listen to each other, managing tension and conflict while not superficially compromising.

Job Descriptions

Each leadership position entails specific tasks and responsibilities, expectations, and relationships. These should be clearly expressed in realistic job descriptions for every paid and nonpaid position, and understood by all persons involved. These job descriptions state the reasons for the job, the requirements, the relationships involved, the responsibilities, and the resources, including training and support.

Job descriptions are not to be used legalistically, but cooperatively. They clarify expectations, foster communication, and build relationships. They are used in recruiting and in evaluation, and are revised for an honest description of reality.

Leadership Styles

There is much recent research on leadership behavior styles. How persons function is as significant as what they do. Christian education personnel could improve their attitudes and enhance their effectiveness by using these studies to analyze their leadership styles in Christian education and then adopting behavior appropriate to each situation.

Leadership styles are behavior patterns that persons use when they are working with and through other people, as perceived by those people.[3] Leaders, therefore, should periodically learn how they are perceived, even though accurate feedback is difficult to get.

Some studies depict leadership styles on a continuum from *authoritarian* (concern for tasks) to *nondirective democratic* (concern for human relationships). Differences in styles are frequently related to the leader's assumptions about human nature and about personal authority. The range of styles and source of authority are depicted in a chart by Robert Tannenbaum and Warren H. Schmidt.[4]

Some studies indicate not one continuum but various combinations, including both task-oriented and relationships-oriented behaviors. Many leadership workshops and training materials use the Managerial Grid developed by Robert R. Blake and Jane S. Mouton[5] or its combination with the Ohio State leadership quadrants by which a leader's style may be charted and compared with five identified styles.[6]

No one style of leadership is best for all circumstances. Two rather extreme leaders who usually cause negative consequences in church administration are an *autocratic executive* (who directs, monitors, and controls) and an *abdicator* (who makes assignments and leaves people alone). In many situations, especially in church activities, the most

Continuum of Leader Behavior

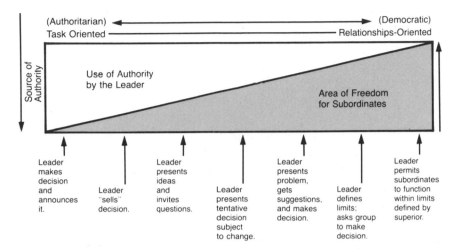

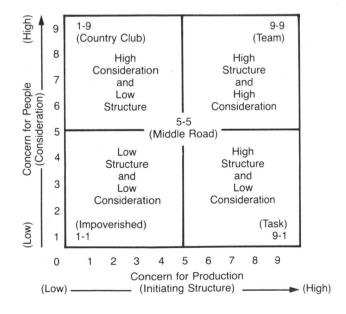

Merging of the Ohio State and the
Managerial Grid Theories of Leadership

effective styles have fairly high concerns both for people and for tasks, with an emphasis on people concerns. Different styles are needed for different situations and activities.

The most appropriate leadership behavior of a Sunday school superintendent toward an adult class that likes to choose its own topics and resources is different from the leadership style toward an insecure new teacher who requests help for a discipline problem.

At least four major variables affect the preferred leadership style:

- The characteristics of the leader;
- The attitudes and needs of the followers;
- The characteristics of the organization (this congregation and this educational group);
- The conditions in the immediate situation.

Since it is impractical to change leaders continually, it follows that leaders will need to adapt different styles at different times and get appropriate feedback and evaluation so as to make appropriate adjustments. The two key ingredients for adapting an effective leadership style are the maturity and needs of followers and the ability of the leader to adjust to these.

The concept of adaptive leadership style corresponds with the biblical model of servant leadership, giving priority to the needs of people and to the will of God, rather than desiring to be served. Servant leadership does not mean being wishy-washy, but adaptive, purposeful, situational, and willing to take risks. The model servant leader was Jesus, whose actions and words showed that leadership is ministry, working with people in their situations, enabling them to serve and manifest the kingdom of God.

Leadership Development

Preparation for leadership does not begin when a new youth adviser is needed and we look for someone to recruit. It is already happening when children and adults have experiences with leaders and grow in leadership skills by accepting and developing increasing responsibility both for themselves and for the mission of the church.

Leadership development is the entire congregation's responsibility. An aspect of the congregation's purpose and life-style is to help every person grow into mature discipleship, into the measure of the stature of Christ, in responsible utilization of God's gifts. The congregation's "climate" and life profoundly affect leadership and its development. Usually specific responsibility for leadership development in Christian education is given to the Christian education committee so that goals and actions are carried out. A natural tendency in church administration is to do those tasks that need immediate attention, such as deciding and ordering curriculum materials for a confirmation ministry class that begins next month. It is just as important, though frequently neglected, to work toward long-range goals, especially nurturing potential leaders and developing leadership skills in present workers.

Leadership development is enabling persons to minister in and through specific jobs in the church's mission. In every congregation there should be plans and activities in these seven areas:

1. Identifying job needs and tasks to be done;
2. Establishing standards and expectations for each position or task;
3. Identifying persons with gifts and potential for varieties of service;
4. Matching and recruiting these persons;
5. Motivating them, unleashing that within persons which incites them to their best work;
6. Equipping leaders with resources, assistance, training, and support;
7. Evaluating the job description, the conditions, the experiences, and the results, with both affirmation and indications for improvement. Evaluation and intentional improvement are important, but frequently avoided in church life. Many leaders are unaware of their leadership styles or of the effects or even of their work. Responsible stewardship and improved motivation involve accountability, maturity in discipleship, evaluation, and "speaking the truth in love." Either "speaking the truth" or "loving," one without the other, may be detrimental.

Leadership development is time consuming, is never completed, and is not easy. Jesus expended much energy and a great amount of time preparing his disciples to be leaders, giving them much personal attention and instruction. Unfortunately, far too many leaders in the church today are hastily assigned a responsibility, given brief instructions, and left on their own. This should not happen to anyone, including the pastor. Any responsibility important enough to be done is important enough to be evaluated, and the person doing it deserves supportive supervision.

Most religious denominations have leadership-training resources— manuals, workshop designs, media materials, and experienced personnel. But it is up to the congregation to use these and develop their own ways of calling and equipping the saints for a variety of ministries. Everything the church does is dependent on this continuing task of leadership development.

Motivating

Leadership development and many leadership functions involve motivating people, including oneself. Motivation is the working of God's Spirit within people, as well as their inner desires and drives. Other persons and conditions do not cause motivation, but have significant effect on that within a person which reinforces or inhibits attitudes and behavior.

There are many studies, books, and manuals related to motivating persons in church activities that Christian education leaders would do well to use both in understanding themselves and in improving their ministries.

Persons are motivated to serve when they:

1. feel they are being treated as persons;
2. feel they are making a contribution;
3. feel what they are doing is in some way serving Jesus Christ (Christian vocation);
4. feel appreciated by somebody;
5. have a good self-image, confidence in their ability;
6. understand what is expected of them;
7. have the ability to do what is expected;
8. see results, evidence of accomplishment soon;
9. feel teamwork, belonging to others who are also involved, and they with them;
10. feel some recognition, reward, or status;
11. have a sense of the importance of this task or job;

12. have and feel support;
13. find challenge, stimulation, excitement, or fun;
14. understand and fit into the system;
15. understand and agree with the aims and purposes of the system (congregation and specific agency or activity of the church);
16. sense that God is working through them.

Numbers 2, 4, 8, and 9 reflect an orientation toward others, liking people.

Numbers 2, 3, 8, and 11 are service oriented.

Numbers 4, 9, 11, 12, and 14 are related to friends or support.

Numbers 5, 6, 7, 10, 13, and 16 are related to personal fulfillment.

Numbers 2, 3, 11, 15, and 16 show identity with significant causes.

The Pastor's Role in Christian Education

Although most leadership in a congregation is done by members as part of their lay ministries, the pastor is the key leader, whose attitude and actions have profound effect. Pattison sees the pastor as essentially a shepherd of systems and identifies leadership as the first function of a strong, living system, such as the church.[7] The pastor, whose being and doing go together, nurtures and guides the subsystems of the church and is part of the Christian education subsystem.

What is the pastor's role in Christian education, what does the pastor do, and how does he or she do it? Interviews and articles indicate both variety and similarities.[8] Some pastors demean Christian education by giving it very little of their time and concern, communicating thereby that it is not important. Some spend as much as one-fourth of their time involved with Christian education, including administration, and with over 120 hours a year actual teaching time.[9] Others consider most of their ministry as related to equipping the laity for their ministries in daily life, with an emphasis on adult education.

The pastor's relationship with Christian education in most situations can be described in eight general roles, with variations as to specific tasks and styles.

1. Educator/theorist

Being aware of all aspects of church life, the pastor visualizes, interprets, and integrates Christian education with the whole life of the congregation, especially its worship, witness, and service, and also with the denomination. Understanding both faith development, Christian nurture, and how persons learn and change, the pastor conceptualizes a practical philosophy of Christian education that is both theologically valid and educationally sound, communicates this with other leaders, and helps see that Christian education activities, methods, and resources reflect this.

2. Teacher

The chief representative teacher in the congregation is probably the pastor, who regularly teaches communion instruction, confirmation classes, new member classes, and Bible studies, and also occasionally teaches in Sunday school, retreats, and other settings. Much teaching is done in connection with pastoral care, baptisms, weddings, funerals, and informal visitations. Pastors also teach teachers and other congregational leaders, individually and in groups, in committee meetings, informal settings, or leadership classes.

3. Learner

Pastors learn while being the leaders in the various settings listed and also by being participants in other congregational and community groups. Continuing education opportunities are vital, as is private reading and study.

4. Theological interpreter

The pastor provides biblical and theological insight and application not only through preaching and teaching but also in church administration, pastoral care, and community activities.

5. Administrative partner

The pastor works cooperatively with the other educational leaders, especially participating as a member (but not chair) of the Christian education committee, performing various appropriate administrative functions, such as goal setting, decision making, evaluation, and leadership development.

6. Leadership developer

The gifts and skills of members are frequently recognized by the pastor, and these are developed by sharing responsibility, affirming ministries, motivating, providing training, giving support, and being an available resource.

7. Pastor of persons

Pastors are expected to care for people, individually and in groups, serving as pastor to the children and youth as well as adults. Personal concern for those who serve as leaders—and not merely for their work—is important.

8. Model

This is not another role but is manifested in all of the above. The pastor's attitude, activities, and style are seen as an example of faith, discipleship, and leadership—whether or not one agrees with that model.

The specific tasks, priorities, and styles of a pastor vary with differing times, settings, and persons, usually according to the desires, habits and abilities of the pastor, the crying demands in the congregation, and the emerging needs and concerns of the congregation and community. No pastor can do all that she or he would like to do in Christian education or satisfy the expectations of all the members. Therefore, periodic evaluation and prioritization of roles and tasks is needed, based on what is best for the congregation at that time under those conditions.

Changes in tasks, priorities, or style of the pastor are appropriate, but may be disruptive unless agreed on by partners in leadership and other persons affected by the changes. In many situations the attitude and relational behavior are more important than the specific tasks done.

Other Professional Staff

An increasing number of congregations are able to add a staff member who has professional training in Christian education and is called by the congregation to serve primarily in areas related to Christian education and youth ministry. There are various titles, including associate in ministry, director of Christian education, or minister of education. These staff members carry out many of the leadership functions and roles described in this chapter, but they are not the primary doers of Christian education. They assist, counsel, and equip the congregation's educational leaders and committee in doing their responsibilities. There should be a detailed written job description for each staff position, approved by the church council and pastor, and reviewed annually.

God's Work

Leadership in Christian education is ministry, servant leadership, and serving God by interacting with people doing God's mission in the world. Improved techniques, efficient management, goal setting, and evaluation are appropriate means, but they are not the primary concern. That concern is to minister—to serve God and help the people of God responsibly fulfill the church's mission. Nurture in the Word and growth in grace and discipleship are basic for developing and sustaining leadership. The magnificent miracle is that God calls and enables people to be his ambassadors, living in us, and through us continuing his creative and redemptive and sanctifying work in the world.

TWELVE

INTO THE FUTURE WITH CHRISTIAN EDUCATION

Arnold D. Weigel

Evident in the preceding chapters is the conviction that Christian education is a multidimensional process of reception, inquiry, discovery, remembrance, affirmation, interpretation, and reinterpretation within the community of faith, centered in Christ and with a sensitivity to relating faith and life creatively and meaningfully. This process is simultaneously a gift and a responsibility, as together we explore the frames of human relationship with God personalized in Christ Jesus and lived in the community of faith.

While previous chapters have addressed particular perspectives of this multidimensional process within the church and the world, this chapter will focus primarily on the future. It is impossible today for us not to think of the future. In this chapter it will be less my intent to project a future than it will be to try to clarify a pathway into the future. In that effort, I will speak about fears, faith, and the future, noting in particular how Martin Luther exemplified some sound insights in correlating fears and future through a living faith in God. Using the well-known Reformation hymn, "A Mighty Fortress Is Our God," I shall identify some key agenda items as we move into the future. Keeping in mind that the congregation is a basic locus for Christian nurture and ministry, with both "in-reach" and outreach centered in the congregation's worship life, I shall identify some chief concerns in planning for the congregation's future, both structurally and functionally, in Christian education. Realizing that no one "is an island, entire of itself," with this truth equally applicable to us as individuals and as organizations, I shall briefly point to intercongregational, interorganizational, and ecumenical possibilities in fostering a growing collegiality in undertaking the responsibilities and in celebrating the gifts intrinsic to the multidimensional process of Christian education.

Fears, Faith and the Future

In this chapter, Christian education is defined as a process of helping us face our fears *of* the future as well as our fears *for* the future with a dynamic, responsible, and confident faith in the triune God. While this faith comes from hearing the Word of God and participating actively in the faith community, we readily acknowledge with educator Thomas Groome: "The very journey to maturity of faith itself demands a struggle and a certain 'wrestling.' To come to religious identity requires that we wrestle, like Jacob of old, with ourselves, with our past, with our present, with our future, and even with our God."[1]

This wrestling of which Groome so emphatically speaks must be at the level of the foundational issues and questions posed by the enterprise itself. Of course, our means of appropriating and our ways of responding will vary from one point on our pilgrimage to another, but the issues are abiding. In this I am reminded of the words of one of my favorite high-school English teachers, who usually started her course on Shakespeare by saying, "There really isn't anything new under the sun. We'll discover this as we explore and appreciate the wisdom of Shakespeare. It's just that it's coming at us in new, different, and accelerated ways."

What this English teacher did in helping students appreciate Shakespeare and use this literature to better understand life and the world is precisely what we are called on to do as Christian educators with the biblical literature, wrestling with past, present, future, and even with God.

I have the students in my Christian education class turn to Luke 24:1-49 and explore this passage from the perspective of correlating fears and future through faith in the living God. In the process the students note that there is an emphasis on *remembering*,[2] on Jesus the Christ in our midst through the breaking of the bread and through study of the Scriptures, and on *witnessing*—"You are witnesses of these things. And behold, I send the promise of my Father upon you; but stay in the city, until you are clothed with power from on high" (vv. 48-49).

Not long ago I heard a botanist say, "A tree's ability to withstand the storms of winter is determined in large measure by the depth and the spread of its root system." This is a fitting analogy for us as we face a turbulent present—turbulent with anxieties, phobias, violences, to name but a few—and a fearful future.[3] It is said that the strength with which we are capable of facing the future is determined by where we have been and where we are, by how we have been and how we are. That is to say, our capacity to face the future is in large measure determined by how firmly rooted we are in the community of faith, by how significantly we interact with important remnants from the past, by how intimately we relate to treasured traditions from the past and in the present. The book of Proverbs tells us, "Where there is no vision, the people perish" (29:18 KJV). But to have that vision, there needs to be a creative wrestling with the past and the present.

As a pilgrim people, engaged in a pilgrimage whose destiny is not yet defined except by promise, we stand in faith before God's throne, believing God's gracious promises for the future.[4] We participate in the activities of the faith community, experiencing these through Word and sacrament as a foretaste of what God has promised us into eternity. We realize that "the old *content* of faith—the same yesterday, today and forevermore—is always received under the conditions of a new *context* of life."[5] As such, we are constantly called on to respond to the question: "What does it mean to be a Christian in this place at this time?" In one of his prison letters, the theologian and martyr Dietrich Bonhoeffer put the question this way: "What is bothering me incessantly is the question what Christianity really is, or indeed who Christ really is for us today."[6]

When Martin Luther was asked what he would do if he knew the world were to end tomorrow, he answered: "I would go out and plant a tree today." For Luther, God's self-revelation in Jesus the Christ was sufficient to meet all quests for the meaning of life. In many respects, I believe that Luther was voicing what Sam Keen meant when he said, "Hope is a memory of the future"[7] or what Paul Ricoeur meant in saying, "Hope is the same thing as remembering."[8]

Proleptic eschatology

What Luther emphasized in his bold declaration of faith was a firm confidence in God's trustworthiness. It was the conviction that, "for Christians, it is time to develop a theology and an action plan so that our churches do not merely try to cope with our own problems, but, more important, strive to become a creative force as the present generation confronts the challenges of tomorrow."[9] This position relative to the future is identified as that of "proleptic eschatology," which is based on the promise of God's future fulfillment of all things revealed in the Bible, inspired by the proclamation of the gospel, that by God's grace the destructive power of human sin will be overcome, providing an exciting vision of the new world toward which all humankind should be striving, and releasing the transforming power of the final future into the present moment.[10]

Proleptic living means that we consciously seek our identity in relation to the coming kingdom of God. In this way the future becomes present in us, even as God was incarnate in Christ. He is the future made in us. As God raised him to new life in the resurrection, so also will God raise us to new life and will transform the present world of nature and history. Our life of faith can be proleptic too. As we place our faith in Christ and are united with him, the transforming power of God's future is loosed in our lives. We become a force, an agent, a means for newness, even while we live in the present. Such faith will enable us to face the fears *of* the future and *for* the future with confidence. Such faith will strengthen us to assist others in facing those same fears with a dynamic creativity.

To speak of "proleptic eschatology" is not only to speak of a future orientation influencing present activity; it is also to speak of a hope orientation informing and shaping present attitudes and actions. Our faith as Christians is in the God of the future, who has shown himself to be faithful through the ages and trustworthy in the present. Faith founded on the solid rock of the resurrected Christ is a faith that is sufficiently strong to face life's trials and tribulations. The future becomes present in us, just as God was incarnate in Christ Jesus; the hope becomes present in us, just as God raised up Christ Jesus from the dead.

In answer to the question, Do we have a future? we are able to say in faith: "Yes, indeed!" God has promised us a future—not simply a future but a future blessed by his presence: "Lo, I am with you always" (Matt. 28:20). "The future is in our imaginations and with God. In that conviction is our hope."[11]

An Agenda for the Future

The old contents of the Christian faith are received in everchanging and new contexts. Ours is a new age, defined by futurologists as "Information Society"; this is Alvin Toffler's "Third Wave"[12] and John Naisbitt's "megashift."[13] This is not just a trend, but a shift; it is leaving one world and entering another.

Seymour and Miller say, "Christian Education continually faces the question of the context within which the church must exist and the meaning of the faith within that context."[14]

When Martin Luther wrote *The Large Catechism* and *The Small Catechism* in 1529, he took that which was considered basic to the Christian tradition and explored the fundamental question, What does this mean? What Luther expressed in the catechisms has endured through the centuries.

> The Small Catechism is one of those deceptively simple works that has a way of getting to the depths of things just because it is so simple. A person can learn it as a child, as generations of Lutherans have, and then come back to it as an adult to discover that it has a fresh and vital way of cutting through complexities to the nub of life.[15]

Perhaps equal to the catechisms in appeal and significance for Lutherans is the hymn "A Mighty Fortress Is Our God." Throughout the world Lutherans sing this hymn as an identity symbol and as a hearty proclamation of particular treasured theological interpretations since the days of the Reformation. I shall be using specific lines of this hymn to identify some agenda items for the future.[16]

Although this listing is in no way exhaustive but only suggestive, and perhaps a catalyst for the reader to add further agenda items, it does signify the necessity through Christian education to rediscover our treasured traditions, to interpret them in the light of present contexts, and to add our own insights and activities to those traditions.

"A mighty fortress is our God"*

Theological, ecclesiological and pedagogical concerns are highlighted by this first line. Who is God for us? What image or images of the church are significant for us? With what implications for worship? for education? for service? for witness? for support?

Through the Apostles' Creed (and Luther's profound explanation), we profess a firm faith in God the Creator, God the Redeemer, and God the Sanctifier—yet one God. We affirm a living interdependence with God's created world, and we acknowledge a readiness to stand in the biblical traditions, which declare God's abiding love and our responsibilities in sharing that love. Yet even amidst this the questions persist: Who is God for us as we move into the 21st century? How do we relate our belief in God in a world of religious pluralism?

"A mighty fortress is our God" also raises ecclesiological questions: How do we view the church? By what image of the church do we engage in ministry? How do we view the church's role in society? Is the church an agent for social transformation in society? Or is it a fortress, an escape from the world?

Luther was emphatic that we are "little Christs"—incarnations of God's love in the world. Seymour and Miller say, "Christian education must continue to address questions about the agenda for Christian mission and vocation—questions raised by the present situation of the world, with its hunger, oppression, and gap in wealth—and about how to speak the Christian message meaningfully and powerfully in this cultural context."[17]

---

*Hymn text © 1978 Lutheran Book of Worship

Much is said today about "theological reflection"—that is, the raising of the "God questions" in our everyday experiences.[18] To speak of "A mighty fortress is our God" is to raise that pedagogical question. How does one teach to generate faith commitment in Christ which will result not in a privatized faith but in a public faith of servanthood? How does one teach to foster an interpretive approach that brings together creatively and meaningfully tradition, culture, and experience? How might one employ computer technology, geared to the gathering and manipulating of factual data, for the generation of faith commitment in learners and teachers? Education programs of insight and correlation—like *Word and Witness* and *Search Weekly Bible Studies*—rather than answering these questions, alert us to the need of asking them ever anew in changing contexts.

In a world of many sovereign nations in a world of superpowers, in a world fearful of, yet enamored by, military strength and might, what does it mean to say: "A mighty fortress is our God?" What does it mean to the church? to the Lutheran church? to Christian education?

"No strength of ours can match his might"

In an age of self-sufficiency, insatiable consumerism, and rampant militarism, one wonders whether we really believe that "no strength of ours can match his might."

We readily know what Luther had in mind when he penned this line. He was testifying to our inability to do successful battle with life's powers and principalities. He was expressing to his inestimable faith in Christ Jesus as the Lord of life. He was acknowledging that on our own we stand condemned before the law.

But we are living in a world in which submission to God's will, acknowledgment of our creatureliness, admission of our sinfulness is questioned and often termed unnecessary. We have come to treasure self-sufficiency and independence. The might of humankind—whether measured in knowledge acquired, wealth amassed, arms built up, or properties held—although feared by some, is honored and highly revered by many.

Yet when it comes to Christian education, we dare not forget the message of the prophets and the apostles. "Cursed is the man who trusts in man and makes flesh his arm, whose heart turns away from the Lord. He is like a shrub in the desert, and shall not see any good come. He shall dwell in the perched places of the wilderness, in an uninhabited salt land. Blessed is the man who trusts in the Lord, whose trust is the Lord. He is like a tree planted by water, that sends out its roots by the stream, and does not fear when heat comes, for its leaves remain green, and is not anxious in the year of drought, for it does not cease to bear fruit" (Jer. 17:5-8). "For all who are led by the Spirit of God are sons of God. . . . It is the Spirit himself bearing with our Spirit that we are children of God, and if children, then heirs, heirs of God and fellow heirs with Christ, provided we suffer with him in order that we may also be glorified with him. . . . For I am sure that neither death, nor life, nor angels, nor principalities, nor things present, nor things to come, nor powers, nor height, nor depth, nor anything else in all creation, will be able to separate us from the love of God in Christ Jesus our Lord" (Rom. 8:14, 16-17, 38-39). But how is this message to be proclaimed so as to be heard in an age of self-sufficiency and self-reliance?

"Though hordes of devils fill the land"

Many of our fears of the future and for the future are motivated and informed by "hordes of devils" that fill not only our land, but the world, including our hearts, our attitudes, our relationships, our social structures and systems—hordes of devils all ready to devour us. We are filled with "an apocalyptic dread."[19] In many respects, the threat of nuclear holocaust, the devastating and alarming increase of acid rain, and the ever-growing spread of terrorism and violence have all given specific detail to Armageddon's ferocity and to its horror. "If *God* is doing Armageddon, it is controlled and with a purpose. But if Armageddon is *man's* act, then it is uncontrolled and without purpose. I think it is this which makes for apocalyptic dread."[20]

"We tremble not." This is very questionable. Surely in the midst of this, the ministry of the congregation in its fullness—but especially in its educational ministry—is to enable us to get in touch with our fears and to explore the social and personal issues impacting on life in the world, particularly the lives of marginalized people. Therefore an agenda for the future in the midst of the "hordes of devils" must surely be for the church to recover its historic commitment to social transformation. This does not mean forgetting personal transformation; rather, it means that the individual agenda must be balanced with the attention to the social context for learning, as well as to our responsibility to the wider world. It means facing with a goal towards becoming better informed and equipped, issues of war and peace, violence, terrorism, homosexuality, regionalism, and the land and environment within the context of the congregation. It means searching the Scriptures together in the community of faith as a means for understanding and empowerment.

A further agenda grows out of this: the church must recover its sense of reformation. In *The Vindication of Tradition,* Jaroslav Pelikan begins with an anecdote from Richard Altman's story of how *Fiddler on the Roof* evolved from the stories of Sholom Aleichem into the Broadway musical and worldwide success it eventually became: "I don't know who finally made the discovery that the show was really about the disintegration of a whole way of life, but I do remember that it was a surprise to all of us. And once we found that out—which was pretty exciting—[Jerome] Robbins said, *'Well if it's a show about tradition and its dissolution, then the audience should be told what that tradition is.'* . . . *'Tradition'* was the key to *Fiddler's* meaning."[21] Isn't tradition also the key to the meaning of the Christian church, to what it means to being a Lutheran in this place at this time? We too need to be told what that tradition is.

"God's Word forever shall abide"

It is no accident that this great Lutheran hymn sounds a firm note of assurance and acceptance and places a central emphasis on the Word of God. So it was in Luther's own life and ministry. Appearing before his accusers at the Diet of Worms, Luther declared: "My conscience is captive to the Word of God. I cannot and I will not recant anything, for to go against conscience is neither right nor safe. God help me. Amen."

The Lutheran Confessions define the church as "the assembly of all believers among whom the Gospel is preached in its purity and the holy sacraments are administered according to the Gospel" (Augsburg Confession #7). The Lutheran tradition has placed a strong emphasis on God's Word abiding forever. Education permeates the whole ministry of the congregation in an effort to interpret this conviction in word and deed, and to be interpreted by it.

Two interrelated agenda items for the future emerge from this emphasis.

Sacramental imagination

First, there is the need to identify, nurture, and develop a "sacramental imagination."[22] This is not idle wonderment about the future. Instead, the exercising of sacramental imagination "must be a creative and shaping activity that gives intentionality to the future as it arises out of the present and the past. Imagination involves a refusal to duplicate what is given or to take the shape of the future as inevitable. It looks from the present to the future to envision the consequences of present action and returns from the future to shape the present in the direction of what might be preferred consequences."[23]

To speak of "sacramental imagination" is to apply an interpretive perspective of sacramentality to all of life. It is to ask: How is God present to me in today's world? How am I present for God in today's world? In a more specific way, it also speaks about our human need to participate regularly in God's sacrament of Eucharist. It is also to ask whether for us Lutherans the sacrament of Baptism can continue to be primarily for infants. Given the age in which we live, we need to ask whether infant Baptism should continue to be normative, or whether adult Baptism, as was the case in the pre-Constantinian Church, should become more customary.[24] We live in an age in which increasing and concentrated attention needs to be paid to the adult catechumenate.

Catechesis

Second, there is the need to reexplore the meaning of the word *catechesis,* which comes from the Greek verb *katechein* and means "to resound, to echo or to hand down." Literally it means "oral in-struction." The etymology of the word implies an oral instruction. It is used in the New Testament as an oral instruction in which a very simple explanation (one step beyond the *kerygma*) was given to the people, as milk rather than solid food is given to small children (see Hcb. 5:12-14; 1 Cor. 3:1-3). The message was to be taught and spoken accurately (Acts 18:25). This understanding of catechesis continued in the early church, where it was understood as a verbal exhortation to live a moral life.[25] Catechesis is basically the activity of "echoing" or retelling the story of Christian faith; it is thus a specific and ongoing instructional activity within the ministry of the Christian congregation. Within the Lutheran tradition we have a long history of catechetical instruction, but it is a history that needs to focus less on the institutionalized structures than on the historical roots of the enterprise. If the Word of God is to abide forever, then the whole congregation needs to assume accountability for its catechizing ministry. "One generation shall laud thy works to another, and shall declare thy mighty acts" (Ps. 145:4).

When we speak of God's Word abiding forever, we need to remember that our task is less one of conservation than it is of *proclamation,* less one of preservation than it is one of *declaration.* We love because he first loved us (1 John 4:10-12).

Planning for the Congregation's Future in Educational Ministry

Where does one begin? I shall begin with a local ministerium, that had agreed to read Lyle Schaller's *Looking in the Mirror* and to use his analytical approach at their subsequent meeting with reference to Christian education in the parish.[26]

The six people who responded for the next meeting discovered that very quickly they got involved in discussing the present status of and future directions for Christian education in the parish setting. In turn each person offered some perceptive analysis.

Pastor 1 said, "I don't really care what Schaller says, I'm frustrated with Christian education. In our parish, we virtually deprive our Sunday school teachers and pupils of any opportunity to worship. With Sunday school at the same time as worship, we have basically a schooling approach without any connection to worship. We're heavy on information but light on experience."

Pastor 2 was quick to respond with what appeared like a solution, saying, "We have wrestled with that problem for years. Now we have our pupils and staff attend Sunday school for three Sundays each month, and on the fourth Sunday, they attend the full worship service. If there is a fifth Sunday, that is used for a discussion of experiences in worship the previous Sunday."

Pastor 3 was pleased that in her three-point parish Sunday school was being held in each congregation at a time other than worship. "This allows for regular participation in both education and liturgy and provides for the inclusion of a fairly active adult Bible-study group in each congregation," according to the pastor.

Both Pastors 4 and 5 said that as far as they were concerned, "There really is no need for Sunday school. The emphasis should be on worship and participation in worship; this goes for children as well as adults. Such an emphasis would allow rituals, stories, images, and practices to serve an educational purpose."

Pastor 6 noted excitement by both "realities and possibilities in Christian education," maintaining that all of the church's ministry is Christian education. In fact, the pastor said, "One of the traps is that we have limited Christian education to the formal schooling approach, but to do so is to do a disservice to both education and ministry. Both education and ministry have a their primary focus to help people grow in faith. And this may happen through worship, through school, through work or play, through study."

Intentionality in planning

What is evident from this discussion is that the structuring, the format, and the process of Christian education in the parish setting is negotiable. The responsibility is not. Because many congregations are small and probably will continue to be small, how is the educative responsibility best fulfilled within the congregational structures and context? This requires planning.

As this planning for participation is exercised, there are questions that should be considered in that process: What does the Bible demand of us? What does the tradition expect of us? What does the context call for? What do we hope for and desire? How do we work toward that? With whom do we work toward that?

Obviously there needs to be a committee under the church council in charge of this planning. But somehow the educational ministry should be directly related to the congregation's mission statement. The planning needs to take seriously the creative correlation of *vision, climate,* and *action* of the congregation, with an eye both to the immediate and long-term future.

The congregation is a basic and a vital locus for educational ministry, and will continue to be so into the future. Of course, it will take planning and intentionality for the congregation to *feel* and to *be* generative as a vital agent for Christian ministry in a bewildering and searching world. The congregation's primary emphasis will need to be on the nurture of meaningful belonging and on empowerment for service. Initiation, maintenance, growth, and empowerment will be key concepts and components in this vital ministry.

Educational ministry, of whatever strata or format, needs to have built into it the opportunity for dialog. "Dialogue is necessary for building Christian community within the group. . . . Two essential activities are constitutive of dialogue, telling and listening."[27] It is also asking, Where can I get help, guidance, and strength to deal with life's crushing problems and devastating fears?

In an Adult Ministries Consultation held in 1984, Jean Haldane stated that in the church, as well as in the world, we are all too ready to be consumers, with the laity being dependent on the clergy for growth and development. She appropriately offers another alternative, which pleads for active adult education as a forum of dialog.

If the church is to be more in line with God's agenda, which is to reconcile the whole world to himself, then it must take seriously Jesus' proclamation of the kingdom and his prayer that the kingdom come. In other words, if Christians are to follow that great movement of God into the world, then perhaps a better image for us is "a people on the move"; and a better organizing principle for congregational life is "a laboratory for the kingdom."

If the "real" world is where God is establishing the kingdom, then the church should be a place to figure out, with all the imagination at our disposal, how to enable and how to support the people who are part of, and are helping build, that kingdom.

Then congregations would have educational processes that help lay people uncover their own faith and spirituality and move to greater maturity and more effective ministry. . . . All this assumes learning in community, small groups within the larger congregation where men and women can experience support for growth and development. This is where they are together, not as a band of volunteers for the church, but as a band of ministers for the kingdom.[28]

Shaping the Church's Educational Ministry

It is often assumed that the responsibility for the church's educational ministry rests mainly with the church at large or with seminaries. I believe that there has to be another model, and that is for the local congregation, congregations in clusters, judicatories, seminaries to engage in planning and implementation together. It is claimed that "for Christian education to remain a powerful expression of Christian mission in the future attention must be given to three levels: the local church, denominational staff, and academic study."[29] "The gospel itself will be impoverished if the educational efforts of Christians are impoverished. A vital future for the church's educational program will require local, denominational, interdenominational, and academic cooperation."[30]

In wrestling with how past, present, and future come together meaningfully for us, we need to take seriously what Luther said in his *Large Catechism* in explaining the First Commandment:

It requires that man's whole heart and confidence be placed in God alone, and in no one else. To have God, you see, does not mean to lay hands upon him, or put him into a purse, or shut him up in a chest. We lay hold of him when our heart embraces him and clings to him. To cling to him with all our heart is nothing else than to entrust ourselves to him completely.[31]

John Westerhoff emphasized a similar concern when he said:

Walter Brueggemann, biblical scholar and friend, wrote an essay based on my book *Will Our Children Have Faith?* He entitled it "Will Our Faith Have Children?" by which he meant: "will we be open enough, risking enough, vulnerable enough that God may give us a future that we do not plan or control or connive? Are we able to acknowledge our impotency so that we might receive from God the gift of a future that surprises us?"[32]

God has entrusted to the church the ministry of Word and sacrament. That ministry has a future. In many respects we are its future as we respond to God's call: "Go therefore and make disciples of all nations, baptizing them in the name of the Father and of the Son and of the Holy Spirit, teaching them to observe all that I have commanded you; and lo, I am with you always, to the close of the age" (Matt. 28:19-20).

NOTES

Chapter 1. Roots of Christian Education in North America

1. Lewis J. Sherrill, *The Rise of Christian Education* (New York: Macmillan, 1953), pp. 18-21.
2. Ibid., pp. 22-23.
3. Ibid., p. 53.
4. Ibid., pp. 144-150.
5. Carl A. Volz, *Faith and Practice in the Early Church* (Minneapolis: Augsburg, 1983), pp. 103-107. Cf. also Sherrill, *Rise of Christian Education,* pp. 186-193.
6. William B. Kennedy, "Christian Education through History," in *An Introduction to Christian Education,* ed. Marvin Taylor (Nashville: Abingdon, 1966), p. 24.
7. Martin Luther, *To the Councilmen of All Cities in Germany, That They Establish and Maintain Christian Schools,* in *Luther's Works* (hereafter cited as LW), vol. 45 (Philadelphia: Fortress, 1962), p. 353.
8. *Small Catechism,* in *The Book of Concord* (hereafter referred to as BC), ed. Theodore G. Tappert (Philadelphia: Fortress, 1959), p. 338.
9. LW 45, 355.
10. Martin Luther, *A Sermon on Keeping Children in School,* LW 46, 222.
11. LW 46, 242.
12. LW 45, 368.
13. Cf. J. Donald Butler, *Religious Education* (New York: Harper & Row, 1962), p. 37, where he says that Luther confused religious nurture in the church with the secular process of equipping the young for their places in society. Butler did not understand Luther's concept of the two kingdoms.
14. BC 345.
15. Donald R. Heiges, *The Christian's Calling* (Philadelphia: Muhlenberg, 1958), p. 48.
16. Ibid., p. 49.
17. Ibid., p. 50.
18. LW 46, 250.
19. LW 45, 370.
20. LW 45, 371.

21. Gottfried G. Krodel, "Luther and Education," a paper delivered Oct. 26, 1983, Chicago, as part of "1483 and All That: A Celebration of the Birth of Luther and Raphael," p. 15.
22. Norma Everist, "Luther on Education: Implications for Today," *Currents in Theology and Mission* 12 (April 1985): 82-85.
23. LW 34, 336-337.
24. Robert L. Conrad, "Christian Education and Creative Conflict" (Ph.D. thesis, Princeton Theological Seminary, 1975), pp. 135-139.
25. Phillip E. Pederson, ed., *What Does This Mean? Luther's Catechisms Today* (Minneapolis: Augsburg, 1979), p. 22.
26. Arthur C. Repp, *Confirmation in the Lutheran Church* (St. Louis: Concordia, 1964), p. 55.
27. Ibid., p. 66.
28. Ibid., p. 70.
29. Ibid., pp. 76-79.
30. Pederson, p. 26.
31. Stephen A. Schmidt, *Powerless Pedagogues* (River Forest, Ill.: Lutheran Education Association, 1972), p. 22.
32. Stephen A. Schmidt, "American Education: A Lutheran Footnote," *The Lutheran Church in North American Life,* John E. Groh and Robert H. Smith, eds. (St. Louis: Clayton, 1979), p. 177.
33. Ibid., p. 178.
34. Arthur C. Repp, *Luther's Catechism Comes to America* (Metuchen, N.J.: Scarecrow Press, 1982), p. 101.
35. Richard W. Solberg, *Lutheran Higher Education in North America* (Minneapolis: Augsburg, 1985), p. 201.
36. Ibid., p. 253.
37. Ibid., p. 228.
38. Schmidt, *Powerless Pedagogues,* p. 17.
39. Robert W. Lynn and Elliott Wright, *The Big Little School* (Birmingham: Religious Education Press, 1980), p. 31.
40. Schmidt, *The Lutheran Church in North American Life,* p. 185.
41. Schmidt, *Powerless Pedagogues,* p. 185.
42. Ibid. See his description in Chapter 5 of what it means to be a Lutheran teacher in the Lutheran Church–Missouri Synod.
43. Kendig Brubaker Cully, *The Search for a Christian Education: Since 1940* (Philadelphia: Westminster, 1965). Cully documents the shift in thought from religious education to Christian education and the impact it had on the educational enterprise in the churches.
44. Conrad, "Christian Education and Creative Conflict," p. 304, for full description of the creative conflict model. Cf. also Conrad, "How Can People under Thirty Be Taught Law/Gospel Theology?" *Currents in Theology and Mission* June 1982, pp. 167-173.
45. Stephen A. Schmidt, "Teaching the Faith: On the Edge of the 70's," LEA Monograph Series, vol. 1, no. 1 (River Forest, Ill.: Lutheran Education Association, 1971). Schmidt says that law/gospel theology translates into death-and-life issues that can be dealt with in a five-step Lutheran teaching model.

46. Cf. James W. Fowler, *Stages of Faith* (San Francisco: Harper & Row, 1981) for a description of faith stages. Fowler contends that most Americans are at a third-level synthetic-conventional faith, an accepting, unquestioning stage. However, it is my contention that Lutheran theology is at the fifth stage of a conjunctive or paradoxical-consolidative faith, a stage that recognizes the ambiguities and paradoxes of life. Cf. Conrad, "How Can People under Thirty Be Taught Law/Gospel Theology?"

47. Horace Bushnell, *Christian Nurture* (New Haven: Yale University Press, 1947; reprint of 1888 edition). Bushnell, in reaction to an extreme emphasis on conversion, emphasized that Christian parents can raise their children in such a way that they know themselves to be Christian from the beginning.

Chapter 3.   The Learning Community

1. David M. Evans, *The Pastor's Role in a Teaching Church* (Valley Forge, Pa.: Judson, 1983), p. 21.

2. Paul Tillich, *Systematic Theology,* vol. 1 (Chicago: Univ. of Chicago, 1951), p. 46.

3. Letty M. Russell, ed., *Changing Context of Our Faith* (Philadelphia: Fortress, 1985), p. 15.

4. Letty M. Russell, "Partnership in Educational Ministry," *Religious Education,* March–April 1979, p. 143.

5. Günther Bornkamm, *Jesus of Nazareth* (London: Hodder and Stoughton, 1960), p. 79.

6. Tillich, *Systematic Theology,* vol. 1, p. 62.

7. Paul Tillich, "A Theology of Education," in *Theology of Culture* (Fair Lawn, N.J.: Oxford, 1959), p. 154.

Chapter 4.   The Community of Faith As Curriculum

1. In Dietrich Bonhoeffer, *Christ the Center* (New York: Harper & Row, 1960, 1966), we read that the question of "Who Is Christ?" can be asked only when the answer is already present in the church (p. 32). "Teaching about Christ begins in silence. . . . The church's silence is silence before the Word. . . . To speak of Christ means to keep silent; to be silent about Christ means to speak" (p. 27). "Christ is Christ not as Christ in himself, but in his relation to me. His being Christ is being *pro me*" (p. 47). In Bonhoeffer's *Ethics* (New York: Macmillan, 1955) we read, "Formation comes only by being drawn in into the form of Jesus Christ. It comes only as formation in His likeness, as *conformation* with the unique form of Him who was made man, was crucified, and rose again" (p. 18).

2. Randolph Crump Miller, *Education for Christian Living* (Englewood Cliffs, N.J.: Prentice-Hall, 1956). Miller wrote: "The beloved community of Christ is a redemptive community, in which all members know themselves to be sinners in need of forgiveness, and therefore are willing to forgive others in the fellowship" (p. 50). "Within such a group where they know themselves as persons among persons, the grace of God is at work to assist them in self-acceptance and in the service of others" (p. 17).

3. Not only did the people themselves or their leaders doubt the faithfulness of the Israelites, but God's judgment is poignantly displayed in the naming, "And the Lord said, 'Call his name Not my people, for you are not my people and I am not your God' " (Hos. 1:9).

4. "While we were still weak, at the right time Christ died for the ungodly. . . . For if while we were enemies we were reconciled to God by the death of his Son, much more, now that we are reconciled, shall we be saved by his life. Not only so, but we also rejoice in God through our Lord Jesus Christ, through whom we have now received our reconciliation" (Rom. 5:6,10-11).

5. Dietrich Bonhoeffer, *Life Together* (New York: Harper & Row, 1954). "Innumerable times a whole Christian community has broken down because it had sprung from a wish dream. The serious Christian, set down for the first time in a Christian community, is likely to bring with him a very definite idea of what Christian life together should be and try to realize it. But God's grace speedily shatters such dreams. . . . Only that fellowship which faces such disillusionment, with all its unhappy and ugly aspects, begins to be what it should be in God's sight, begins to grasp in faith the promise that is given to it" (pp. 26-27).

6. 1 Cor. 12:12-27. See also rite of Holy Baptism, *Lutheran Book of Worship*. After the children are baptized, the congregation says to them, "We welcome you into the Lord's family. We receive you as fellow members of the body of Christ, children of the same heavenly Father, and workers with us in the kingdom of God" (p. 125).

7. William E. Diehl, *Christianity and Real Life* (Philadelphia: Fortress, 1976).

8. "Congregation as Confirming Community" (Minneapolis: Division for Life and Mission in the Congregation, the American Lutheran Church, 1984).

9. D. Campbell Wyckoff, "What Curriculum Is—and Is Not," in *Always Being Reformed,* ed. John C. Purdy (Philadelphia: Geneva Press, 1985), pp. 38-39.

10. Donald L. Griggs, *Basic Skills for Teachers* (Nashville: Abingdon, 1985).

11. Ibid., pp. 13, 19, 20, 33.

12. Letty M. Russell, *Human Liberation in a Feminist Perspective—A Theology* (Philadelphia: Westminster, 1974), p. 53. See also Russell, *Growth in Partnership* (Philadelphia: Westminster, 1981).

13. Mary C. Boys and Thomas Groome, "Principles and Pedagogy in Biblical Study," chart presented at the Religious Education Association Convention, Toronto, Ontario, November 1979. The approach asks, "What is this Bible which we carry?" and "Who are we who carry it?" and only then, "How, then, shall we teach?"

14. See Paulo Freire, *Pedagogy of the Oppressed* (New York: Herder and Herder, 1970), and Anza A. Lema, *Pedagogical and Theological Presuppositions of Education* (Kowloon, Hong Kong: Lutheran Southeast Asia Christian Education Curricula Committee, 1977).

15. Parker J. Palmer, *The Company of Strangers* (New York: Crossroad, 1983). Palmer explores a methodology of hospitality, allowing the stranger to remain different rather than assuming similarities as people move inward in spirituality and outward to the public life.

16. Norma J. Everist and Nelvin Vos, *Connections* (Philadelphia: Division for Parish Services, Lutheran Church in America, 1985), develops a methodology for laity to theologize in their own worlds.

17. James D. and Evelyn Eaton Whitehead, *Method in Ministry* (New York: Seabury, 1980). In their theological reflection in ministry model, they present a tripolar approach—the tradition, cultural information, and personal experience through the processes of attending, asserting, and deciding (pp. 11-27).

18. See Elisabeth Schüssler Fiorenza, *In Memory of Her* (New York: Crossroad, 1984) for her "Feminist Theological Reconstruction of Christian Origins."

19. Gabriel Moran, "Work, Leisure, and Religious Education," in *Religious Education* 74, no. 2 (March-April 1979). Moran states that society prepares people for their jobs but we need to give attention to "education *by* our jobs." What does our work teach us? (p. 160). See also Gabriel Moran, *Education toward Adulthood* (New York: Paulist, 1979).

20. Letty M. Russell, *Christian Education in Mission* (Philadelphia: Westminster, 1967).

21. Maria Louisa Charlesworth, *Ministering Children,* American Tract Society, ca. 1850. "Let children be trained, and taught, and led aright . . . and they will not be slow to learn that they possess a personal influence everywhere" (from the preface).

22. Norma J. Everist, *Education Ministry in the Congregation* (Minneapolis: Augsburg, 1983), p. 72.

Chapter 6. Education for Evangelization

1. As reported in *Eternity,* January 1980, p. 20.

2. Hale, J. Russell, *Who Are the Unchurched?* (Atlanta: Glenmary Research Center, 1977; San Francisco: Harper & Row, 1980).

3. In one poll, 94% of the unchurched said they felt a person could be a good Christian or Jew without attending a church or synagogue.

4. A 13th category could be added: those people who want a more definitive challenge in a church, a hard call to commitment. Some are repelled by a bland type of church in which all is sweetness and light. The trouble is, some fundamentalist churches *do* offer that "hard call," and frequently it is a perversion of the gospel.

5. Rauff, Edward A., *Why People Join the Church* (Atlanta: Glenmary Home Missioners, 1979).

6. Ibid., p. 155.

7. *Eternity,* January 1980, p. 24.

8. Ibid.

9. Ibid.

10. Ibid.

11. *Evangelization: Mission Trends No. 2,* G. Anderson and T. Stransky, eds. (New York: Paulist; Grand Rapids, Mich.: Eerdmans, 1975), pp. 132-133.

12. Ibid., p. 4.

13. Lischer, Richard, *Speaking of Jesus: Finding the Words for Witness* (Philadelphia: Fortress, 1982), pp. 9-11.

14. Deffner, Donald L., *Please Talk to Me, God!* (St. Louis: Concordia, 1983), p. 109.

15. The summation that follows by James Oldham is used by permission of James Oldham.

Chapter 7.   Human Development and Christian Education

1. Paul Tillich, *Systematic Theology*, vol. 1 (Digswell Place: James Nisbet and Co., 1953), pp. 67-70.
2. Paul Tillich, *Theology of Culture* (New York: Oxford Univ., 1964), p. 205.
3. Jean Piaget, *Six Psychological Studies*, trans. Anita Tenzer (London: Univ. of London, 1968), pp. 5-6.
4. David Elkind, *Children and Adolescents: Interpretive Essays on Jean Piaget*, 3rd ed. (New York: Oxford Univ., 1981), p. 22.
5. Margaret A. Krych, "Communicating Justification to Elementary-Age Children: A Study in Tillich's Correlational Method and Transformational Narrative" (Ph.D. dissertation, Princeton Theological Seminary, 1985), Chaps. 7-10.
6. See, for example, Edward White, Bill Elsom, and Richard Prawat, "Children's Conceptions of Death," *Child Development* 49 (June 1978): 307-310.
7. See Elkind, *Children and Adolescents*, p. 100.
8. As in algebra, for example. Ibid.
9. Ibid., p. 103.
10. See John Stevens Kerr, ed., *Teaching Grades Seven through Ten* (Philadelphia: Parish Life Press, 1980), Part 3.
11. Due to space limitations, we cannot here present the work of researchers who have extended Piaget's work by adding further stages in adulthood that depend on social and emotional factors. The reader is referred to Lawrence Kohlberg's work in moral development and to James Fowler's work in faith development. Interesting research on religious conceptual development has been carried out by Ronald Goldman and more recently by David Elkind. The following books may be most helpful: Lawrence Kohlberg, *Essays on Moral Development*. Vol. 1. *The Philosophy of Moral Development: Moral Stages and the Idea of Justice* (San Francisco: Harper & Row, 1981); James W. Fowler, *Stages of Faith: The Psychology of Human Development and the Quest for Meaning* (San Francisco: Harper & Row, 1981); Ronald Goldman, *Religious Thinking from Childhood to Adolescence* (New York: Seabury, 1964); David Elkind, *The Child's Reality: Three Developmental Themes* (Hillsdale, N.J.: Lawrence Erlbaum Associates, 1978).
12. See Jerome B. Dusek and John F. Flaherty, "The Development of the Self-Concept During the Adolescent Years," *Monographs of the Society for Research in Child Development* 46:4 (serial no. 191, 1981).
13. See n. 11 on Fowler and Kohlberg.
14. For example, Leon McKenzie, *The Religious Education of Adults* (Birmingham, Ala.: Religious Education Press, 1982), pp. 116ff.
15. Linda Jane Vogel has an excellent discussion of older learners in Chapter 1 of her book, *The Religious Education of Older Adults* (Birmingham, Ala.: Religious Education Press, 1984).

Chapter 8.   Christian Education: An Exercise in Interpreting

1. H. Edward Everding Jr., "A Hermeneutical Approach to Educational Theory," in *Foundations for Christian Education in an Era of Change*, ed. Marvin J. Taylor (Nashville: Abingdon, 1976), p. 41.

2. Bernard L. Marthaler, "Socialization As a Model for Catechetics," in *Foundations of Religious Education*, ed. Padraic O'Hare (New York: Paulist, 1978), p. 77.
3. Jack L. Seymour and Carol A. Wehrheim, "Faith Seeking Understanding: Interpretation As a Task of Christian Education," in *Contemporary Approaches to Christian Education*, Jack L. Seymour and Donald E. Miller, eds. (Nashville: Abingdon, 1982), p. 124.
4. Thomas H. Groome, *Christian Religious Education* (San Francisco: Harper & Row, 1980).
5. Douglas E. Wingeier, "Christian Education As Faith Translation," *The Living Light* 14 (Fall 1977): 393-406.
6. John H. Peatling, "Developmental Hermeneutics, or Interpretations Involve Interpreters." Paper delivered at the 1981 Religious Education Association Convention, pp. 3-4.
7. Everding, *Foundations*, p. 42.
8. Ibid.
9. Irving E. Sigel and Rodney R. Cocking, *Cognitive Development from Childhood to Adolescence: A Constructivist Perspective* (New York: Holt, Rinehart and Winston, 1977).
10. Ibid.
11. For one description of the interpretive process, see A. Roger Gobbel, Gertrude G. Gobbel, and Thomas E. Ridenhour, *Helping Youth Interpret the Bible* (Atlanta: John Knox, 1984), pp. 47-59.
12. Quoted material is from the order for Holy Baptism in *Lutheran Book of Worship*, pp. 121-125.
13. For a description of shaping Christian education for adolescents, see Gobbel, Gobbel, and Ridenhour, *Helping Youth*, pp. 60-71.

Chapter 9.   A Lutheran Approach to Teaching

1. BC 337ff.
2. R. Freeman Butts, *A Cultural History of Western Education* (New York: McGraw-Hill, 1955), pp. 207, 229.
3. Ibid.
4. BC 23-96.
5. Ibid.
6. Butts, *A Cultural History*, pp. 228ff.
7. Ibid.
8. Robert Ulich, ed., *Three Thousand Years of Educational Wisdom* (Cambridge: Harvard Univ., 1961), pp. 339ff.
9. Ibid., pp. 480ff.
10. Ibid., pp. 523ff.
11. Harold Burgess, *An Invitation to Religious Education* (Birmingham: Religious Education Press, 1975).
12. Jack Seymour, *et al.*, *Contemporary Approaches to Christian Education* (Nashville: Abingdon, 1982).
13. Thomas Groome, *Christian Religious Education* (San Francisco: Harper & Row, 1980).

14. John Peating, *Religious Education in a Psychological Key* (Birmingham: Religious Education Press, 1981).
15. Carl Braaten, *Principles of Lutheran Theology* (Philadelphia: Fortress, 1983).
16. Ibid., p. 24.
17. *Lutheran Book of Worship*, pp. 57-119.
18. BC 345.
19. Locke E. Bowman Jr., *Teaching Today* (Philadelphia: Westminster, 1980), pp. 163ff.
20. Mary Cove and Larry Mueller, *Regarding Religious Education* (Mishawaka, Ind.: Religious Education Press, 1977), pp. 59-61.
21. David Silvernail, *Teaching Styles As Related to Student Achievement* (Washington: National Education Association, 1979), pp. 4ff.
22. Burgess, *An Invitation*, p. 51.

Chapter 11.   Leadership in Christian Education

1. William R. Lassey and Richard R. Fernandez, *Leadership and Social Change*, 2nd ed. (La Jolla, Calif.: University Associates, 1976), pp. 7-15.
2. Paul Hersey and Kenneth H. Blanchard, *Management of Organizational Behavior: Utilizing Human Resources*, 3rd. ed. (Englewood Cliffs, N.J.: Prentice-Hall, 1977), pp. 83-89.
3. Ibid., p. 135.
4. Ibid., p. 92, adapted from Tannenbaum and Schmidt, "How to Choose a Leadership Pattern," *Harvard Business Review*, March-April 1957, pp. 95-101.
5. Robert R. Blake and Jane S. Mouton, *The Managerial Grid* (Houston: Gulf Publishing, 1964), p. 99.
6. Hersey and Blanchard, *Management*, p. 97.
7. E. Mansell Pattison, *Pastor and Parish: A Systems Approach* (Philadelphia: Fortress, 1977), pp. 22, 50.
8. Richard A. Olson, ed., *The Pastor's Role in Educational Ministry* (Philadelphia: Fortress, 1974), pp. 13-55.
9. Ibid., p. 15.

Chapter 12.   Into the Future with Christian Education

1. Thomas H. Groome, *Christian Religious Education* (San Francisco: Harper & Row, 1980), p. xv.
2. Jaroslav Pelikan, in *The Vindication of Tradition* (New Haven: Yale Univ., 1984), emphasizes a difference between "traditionalism" and the "rediscovery" and "recovery" of tradition. In the hermeneutical process, we are not only rememberers of history, but we are also history-givers/history-makers, adding tradition to tradition.
3. Ted Peters, *Fear, Faith, and the Future* (Minneapolis: Augsburg, 1980) and Marion E. Brown and Marjorie G. Prentice, *Christian Education in the Year 2000* (Valley Forge, Pa.: Judson, 1984).
4. The imagery of "pilgrim people" is employed by many Christian educators to speak not only of the church but also about the process of Christian education.

Thomas H. Groome, *Christian Religious Education,* pp. 14-15; John H. Westerhoff, *A Pilgrim People* (New York: Seabury, 1984); Foster R. McCurley Jr. and John Reumann, *Word and Witness: Understanding the Bible II* (LCA Division for Parish Services, 1977, 1980), pp. 153-171.

5. Carl E. Braaten, *Principles of Lutheran Theology* (Philadelphia: Fortress, 1983), p. x.
6. Dietrich Bonhoeffer, *Letters and Papers from Prison* (London: SCM Press, 1953), p. 91.
7. Sam Keen, *The Passionate Life: Stages of Loving* (San Francisco: Harper & Row, 1983), p. 34.
8. Paul Ricoeur as quoted in Martin Marty, *The Search for a Usable Future* (New York: Harper & Row, 1969), p. 60.
9. Peters, *Fear, Faith, and the Future,* p. 25.
10. Ibid., p. 31.
11. John Westerhoff, *Will Our Children Have Faith?* (New York: Seabury, 1976), pp. 24-25.
12. Alvin Toffler, *The Third Wave* (New York: Bantam, 1980).
13. John Naisbitt, *Megatrends: Ten New Directions Transforming Our Lives* (New York: Warner, 1982).
14. Seymour *et al., Contemporary Approaches to Christian Education,* pp. 162-163.
15. James Nestingen, *Martin Luther: His Life and Teachings* (Philadelphia: Fortress, 1982), p. 43.
16. Seymour et al., *Contemporary Approaches,* pp. 157ff., lists five agendas for the future: (1) Christian education must seek to recover its historic commitment to social transformation; (2) Christian educators must continue to define Christian education as a central yet distinct ministry of the church; (3) the relationship of developmental psychology theory to Christian education must be reconsidered; (4) Christian educators must seek to clarify the relationship of Christian education to the wider learning environment; (5) the foundational relationship of Christian education to both educational theory and theology must be explored continually.
17. Seymour *et al.,* p. 155.
18. James D. Whitehead and Evelyn E. Whitehead, *Method in Ministry: Theological Reflection and Christian Ministry* (New York: Seabury, 1980).
19. Eduard Riegert, professor of homiletics, Waterloo Lutheran Seminary, Waterloo, Ontario, "The Parish in the Age of 1984" (unpublished).
20. Ibid., p. 2.
21. Pelikan, *The Vindication of Tradition,* p. 3.
22. Jack L. Seymour and Robert O'Gorman, *The Church in the Education of the Public* (Nashville: Abingdon, 1984).
23. Groome, *Christian Religious Education,* p. 186.
24. Eugene L. Brand, *Baptism: A Pastoral Perspective* (Minneapolis: Augsburg, 1975), esp. Chap. 6, "Baptism and Faith," pp. 35ff. J. Neil Alexander, teacher of spiritual formation and liturgics, Waterloo Lutheran Seminary, Waterloo, Ontario, identifies the adult catechumenate as a vital means for Christian education into the future. Relative to the adult catechumenate, see: Kenneth F. Pohlmann (Project Coordinator), *A Handbook for Ministry with the Adult Inquirer* (Minneapolis: Augsburg Publishing House, 1986) and Martin E. Marty, *Invitation To Discipleship: Adult Inquirer's Manual* (Minneapolis: Augsburg Publishing House,

1986) with a Leader's Guide, *Invitation To Discipleship* by Kristine L. M. Carlson (Minneapolis: Augsburg Publishing House, 1986).

25. Groome, *Christian Religious Education,* p. 26.

26. Lyle Schaller, *Looking in the Mirror* (Nashville: Abingdon, 1984).

27. Groome, *Christian Religious Education,* pp. 188-189.

28. Jean Haldane, "Faith, Learning and Ministry: Interrelated and Interdependent," *Origins: NC Documentary Service* 14 (Feb. 21, 1985): p. 599.

29. Seymour *et all., Contemporary Approaches,* p. 163.

30. Ibid., p. 164. Cf. Carl E. Braaten, *The Apostolic Imperative* (Minneapolis: Augsburg, 1985), esp. pp. 190-195.

31. BC 366.

32. Westerhoff, *A Pilgrim People,* p. 30.

FOR FURTHER READING

Chapter 1. Roots of Christian Education in North America

Bushnell, Horace. *Christian Nurture*. Twin Books Series. Grand Rapids, Mich.: Baker, 1979. Reprint of 1888 edition.

Groh, John E., and Smith, Robert H., eds. *The Lutheran Church in North American Life*. St. Louis: Clayton, 1979.

Heiges, Donald R. *The Christian's Calling*. Rev. ed. Philadelphia: Fortress, 1984.

Luther, Martin. "To the Councilmen of All Cities in Germany That They Establish and Maintain Christian Schools." *Luther's Works*. Vol. 45. Walther I. Brandt and Helmut T. Lehmann, eds. Philadelphia: Fortress, 1962.

Luther, Martin. "A Sermon on Keeping Children in School." *Luther's Works*. Vol. 46. Robert C. Schultz and Helmut T. Lehmann, eds. Philadelphia: Fortress, 1967.

Lynn, Robert W., and Wright, Elliott. *The Big Little School: Two Hundred Years of Sunday School*. Nashville: Abingdon, 1980.

Painter, F. V. N. *Luther on Education*. St. Louis: Concordia, n.d. Reprint of 1889 edition. (Out of print.)

Pederson, Phillip, ed. *What Does This Mean? Luther's Catechisms Today*. Minneapolis: Augsburg, 1979.

Repp, Arthur C. *Luther's Catechism Comes to America*. Metuchen, N.J.: Scarecrow Press, 1982.

Schmidt, Stephen A. *A History of the Religious Education Association*. Birmingham: Religious Education Press, 1983.

Solberg, Richard W. *Lutheran Higher Education in North America*. Minneapolis: Augsburg, 1985.

Volz, Carl A. *Faith and Practice in the Early Church*. Minneapolis: Augsburg, 1983.

Chapter 3. The Learning Community

Bonhoeffer, Dietrich. *The Cost of Discipleship*. New York: Macmillan, 1963.

Bonhoeffer, Dietrich. *Life Together*. San Francisco: Harper and Row, 1976.

Downs, Thomas. *The Parish as Learning Community*. Mahwah, N. J.: Paulist, 1979.

Little, Sara. *To Set One's Heart: Belief in Teaching in the Church*. Atlanta: John Knox, 1983.

Russell, Letty. *The Future of Partnership*. Philadelphia: Westminster, 1979.

Russell, Letty. *Growth in Partnership*. Philadelphia: Westminster, 1982.

Westerhoff, John., III, and William H. Willimon. *Liturgy and Learning through the Life Cycle*. San Francisco: Harper and Row, 1985.

Wold, Margaret. *The Shalom Woman*. Minneapolis: Augsburg, 1975.

Chapter 5.   Interaction of Faith and Culture

Dodds, E. R. *Pagan and Christian in an Age of Anxiety: Some Aspects of Religious Experience from Marcus Aurelius to Constantine.* New York: Norton, 1970.

Grant, R. M. *Early Christianity and Society.* San Francisco: Harper & Row, 1977. (Out of print.)

Kaye, Bruce N. "Cultural Interaction in the New Testament." *Theologische Zeitschrift* 40(1984): 341-358.

Kee, Howard C. *Christian Origins in Sociological Perspective.* Philadelphia: Westminster, 1980.

Malherbe, Abraham J. *Social Aspects of Early Christianity.* 2nd rev. ed. Philadelphia: Fortress, 1983.

Meeks, Wayne A. *The First Urban Christians: The Social World of the Apostle Paul.* New Haven: Yale Univ., 1984.

Niebuhr, H. Richard. *Christ and Culture.* New York: Harper & Row, 1951.

Nineham, Dennis. *The Use and Abuse of the Bible: A Study of the Bible in an Age of Rapid Cultural Change.* New York: Barnes and Noble, 1976.

Theissen, Gerd. *The Social Setting of Pauline Christianity: Essays on Corinth.* Trans. John H. Schütz. Philadelphia: Fortress, 1982.

Theissen, Gerd. *Sociology of Early Palestinian Christianity.* Trans. John Bowden. Philadelphia: Fortress, 1978.

Chapter 6.   Education for Evangelization

The Continuing Frontier: Evangelism. A collection of articles by Stockwell, Fuerst, Braaten, Arias, Martinson, Burgess, and Hertz. New York: Lutheran Church in America, 1984.

Diehl, William E. *Christianity and Real Life.* Philadelphia: Fortress, 1976.

Diehl, William E. *Thank God, It's Monday!* Philadelphia: Fortress, 1982.

Griffin, Em. *The Mind Changers.* Wheaton, Ill.: Tyndale, 1982.

Hale, J. Russell. *Who Are the Unchurched? An Exploratory Study.* Atlanta, Ga.: Glenmary, 1977.

Lischer, Richard. *Speaking of Jesus: Finding the Words for Witness.* Philadelphia: Fortress, 1982.

Markquart, Edward F. *Witnesses for Christ: Training for Intentional Witnessing.* Minneapolis: Augsburg, 1981.

Mbiti, John S., ed. *Confessing Christ in Different Cultures.* Bossey, Switzerland: WCC Ecumenical Institute, 1977.

Mission Trends series. Multiple authors. New York: Paulist Press; Grand Rapids: Eerdmans.

Padovano, Anthony T. *The Estranged God.* Fairway, Kan.: Andrews, McMeel, & Parker, 1966.

Powell, John. *A Reason to Live! A Reason to Die!* Rev. ed. Niles, Ill: Argus, 1972.

Rauff, Edward A. *Why People Join the Church.* New York: Pilgrim, 1980.

Savage, John S. *The Apathetic and Bored Church Member.* Pittsford, N.Y.: LEAD Consultants, Inc., 1976.

Stubbe, Arlon K. *The Phantom Church: How to Minister to Potential Parish Dropouts.* Philadelphia: Fortress, 1986.

Chapter 7.   Human Development and Christian Education

Elkind, David. *A Sympathetic Understanding of the Child: Birth to Sixteen.* 2nd ed. Boston: Allyn and Bacon, 1974.

Elkind, David. *The Child's Reality: Three Developmental Themes.* New York: Halsted, 1978.

Elkind, David. *Children and Adolescents: Interpretive Essays on Jean Piaget.* 3rd ed. New York: Oxford Univ., 1981.

Fowler, James W. *Stages of Faith: The Psychology of Human Development and the Quest for Meaning.* San Francisco: Harper & Row, 1981.

Fowler, James W. *Becoming Adult, Becoming Christian: Adult Development and Christian Faith.* San Francisco: Harper & Row, 1984.

Gruber, Howard E. and Vonèche, J. Jacques, eds. *The Essential Piaget.* New York: Basic Books, 1977.

Kegan, Robert. *The Evolving Self: Problems and Process in Human Development.* Cambridge, Mass.: Harvard Univ., 1982.

McKenzie, Leon. *The Religious Education of Adults.* Birmingham, Ala.: Religious Education Press, 1982.

Stokes, Kenneth, ed. *Faith Development in the Adult Life Cycle.* New York: Sadlier, 1983.

Vogel, Linda J. *The Religious Education of Older Adults.* Birmingham, Ala.: Religious Education Press, 1984.

Wyckoff, D. Campbell, and Richter, Don, eds. *Religious Education Ministry with Youth.* Birmingham, Ala.: Religious Education Press, 1982.

Chapter 10.   The Administration of Christian Education

Adams, Arthur M. *Effective Leadership for Today's Church.* Philadelphia: Westminster, 1978.

Clarke, Jean. I. *Who, Me Lead a Group?* Minneapolis: Winston, 1983.

Eble, Kenneth E. *The Art of Administration: A Guide for Academic Administrators.* San Francisco: Jossey-Bass, 1978.

Holck, Manfred Jr. *Clergy Desk Book.* Nashville: Abingdon, 1985.

Lee, Harris W. *Theology of Administration: A Biblical Basis for Organizing the Congregation.* Minneapolis: Augsburg, 1981.

Mintzberg, Henry. *The Nature of Managerial Work.* New York: Harper & Row, 1973.

Scheitlin, George, and Gilstrom, Eleanor. *Recruiting and Developing Volunteer Leaders.* Philadelphia: Parish Life Press, 1979.

Wilson, Marlene. *How to Mobilize Church Volunteers.* Minneapolis: Augsburg, 1983.

Chapter 11.   Leadership in Christian Education

Adams, Arthur M. *Effective Leadership for Today's Church.* Philadelphia: Westminster, 1978.

Evans, David M. *The Pastor in a Teaching Church*. Valley Forge, Pa.: Judson, 1983.

Fransen, Paul S. *Effective Church Councils*. Minneapolis: Augsburg, 1985.

Hersey, Paul, and Blanchard, Kenneth H., *Management of Organizational Behavior: Utilizing Human Resources*. 4th ed. Englewood Cliffs, N.J.: Prentice-Hall, 1982.

Lassey, William R., and Sashkin, Marshall, eds. *Leadership and Social Change*. 3rd rev. ed. La Jolla, Calif.: University Associates, 1983.

Lee, Harris W., *Theology of Administration*. Minneapolis: Augsburg, 1981.

Olson, Richard A., ed. *The Pastor's Role in Educational Ministry*. Philadelphia: Fortress, 1974. (Out of print.)

Pattison, E. Mansell. Howard J. Clinebell and Howard W. Stone, eds. *Pastor and Parish: A Systems Approach*. Creative Pastoral Care and Counseling Series. Philadelphia: Fortress, 1977.

Schaller, Lyle E. *Getting Things Done: Concepts and Skills for Leaders*. Nashville: Abingdon, 1986.

Taylor, Marvin J., ed. *Changing Patterns of Religious Education*. Nashville: Abingdon, 1984.

INDEX